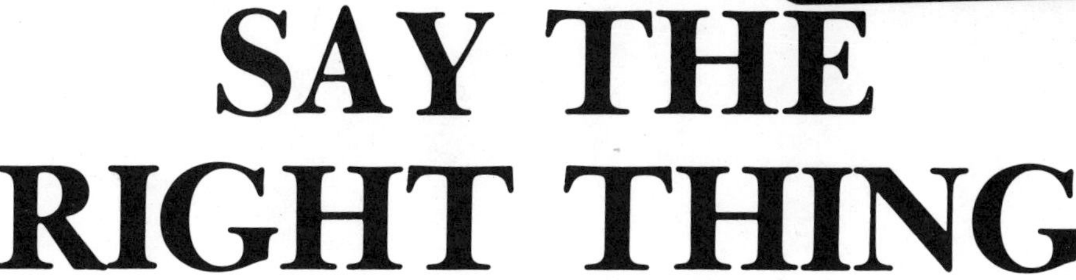

SAY THE RIGHT THING

A Functional Approach to Developing Speaking Skills

CHRISTINE F. MELONI / SHIRLEY THOMPSON / ANDREA BELEY
George Washington University

 ADDISON-WESLEY PUBLISHING COMPANY

Reading, Massachusetts • Menlo Park, California
Don Mills, Ontario • Wokingham, England • Amsterdam
Sydney • Singapore • Tokyo • Madrid • Bogota
Santiago • San Juan

Printed in the United States of America.

ISBN 0-201-10205-6
HIJKLMNOP-DA-99876543210

Acknowledgements

We would like to acknowledge the research carried out by several individuals which has helped us enormously in writing this text. Special thanks are due to our friend, Susan Corsetti, London, Georgetown University, for demonstrating to us the necessity of teaching language functions in the ESL/EFL classroom and for providing us with a framework for developing functional materials. We are also grateful to Andrew D. Cohen, Hebrew University of Jerusalem, and Elite Olshtain, Tel Aviv University, for their cross-cultural studies in the area of apologizing and to Ann Borkin and Susan M. Reinhart, the University of Michigan, for their research dealing with the uses of "I'm sorry" and "Excuse me" by native speakers of American English. The work of Dana Lightman of the University of Pennsylvania in the area of complimenting has also been very useful. The cooperation of Luis Covarrubias in helping to gather data on how American university students give advice was greatly appreciated.

CONTENTS

PREFACE

To the Instructor

PURPOSE

The purpose of this text, which is organized around the concept of language functions, is to increase the learner's communicative competence and performance, that is, the ability to express oneself in a socially as well as grammatically correct way.

The traditional structural approach to language teaching with its emphasis on grammar often leaves the learners knowing a great deal *about* the language but feeling uncomfortable and inadequately prepared to use the language in real life situations.

This text is not intended to replace structural grammar instruction but to supplement it with instruction on how grammar functions in real communication. It is designed to help students do more than form grammatically correct sentences, and to help them judge the social and cultural connotations of their linguistic choices.

INTENDED AUDIENCE

Say the Right Thing is intended for use with students at the intermediate or advanced levels. It assumes the students have been exposed to the core grammatical structures although it does not presuppose mastery of those structures. Since the lessons are centered on language functions, grammar per se is not taught.

At an intermediate or advanced level the text might be used in a variety of ways depending on the particular needs of the students and on the organization of the program.

1. As a supplement to a grammar text
2. As a part of a conversation or speaking/listening component
3. As the basis for a speaking course after the students have completed their formal study of grammar

THE PLACE OF THE FUNCTIONAL APPROACH IN ESL/EFL

In an effort to aid the instructor in deciding whether and where to use this text most effectively, the following background information is provided on how and why these functionally based materials were developed.

To understand the functional approach, it is helpful to define it in relation to two other widely used approaches to organizing language for pedagogical purposes.

The familiar GRAMMAR BASED APPROACH divides language into grammatical units such as "The Past Tense," "Quantifiers," "Noun Clauses," etc. These are taught in what (at least theoretically) is considered the order of difficulty, eventually covering the body of language.

The SITUATIONAL APPROACH bases its divisions on situations such as "Shopping for Food," "Visiting the Doctor," "At the Post Office," etc. The grammar and vocabulary to be taught are derived from the situation.

The FUNCTIONAL APPROACH divides language according to the functions which it serves, such as "Giving Advice," "Greeting People," "Apologizing," "Congratulating," etc. The grammar and vocabulary to be taught consist of whatever is needed to teach the function, although either or both may be limited according to the level of the students.

Most language materials in ESL/EFL combine more than one of these approaches; however, generally, one approach clearly dominates.

THE FUNCTIONAL APPROACH

With these brief descriptions in mind, we can examine in more detail the characteristics of the functional approach.

When the idea of a functional approach to language teaching was first introduced a few years ago, by D.A. Wilkins in particular (*Notional Syllabuses,* 1976), there were many who believed the days of the grammar-based syllabus were, or should be, over. But Wilkins himself did not advocate the total abandonment of the grammar syllabus, although he pointed out its inadequacies. H.G. Widdowson, a strong advocate of the communicative approach to language teaching, regrets that it is widely felt that one must choose between two alternatives since both approaches should be taken into consideration when preparing language teaching materials. This text, therefore, should supplement rather than supplant the teaching of grammar.

The functional approach has added a new dimension to language teaching and it should be considered an essential one because, unlike the grammar approach, it attempts to deal directly with the learner's communicative needs.

Functional materials provide language learners with information which has immediate practical value, such as how to greet people and how to make requests. A functional approach is based on the conviction that what one wants or needs to *do* with language is of primary importance. Thus, it is concerned with the basic purpose of language, communication.

A functional approach to language teaching takes into consideration socio- and psycholinguistic factors such as social roles, attitudes, time, place, and relationships. It provides the learner with basic cultural insights which form the basis for continued learning through observation. Cultural awareness is consequently heightened. While in a grammar-based approach cultural information is incidental, in a functional approach it is essential.

This text offers a means for taking advantage of the new possibilities for language learning offered by a functional approach without necessitating a total curricular restructuring.

We hope that you and your students will find these materials fun, refreshing, and rewarding.

SUGGESTIONS FOR CLASSROOM USE OF THIS TEXT

Student Preparation

The next section, TO THE STUDENT: BEFORE YOU BEGIN, should be gone over carefully with the students before the Units are worked on. It will orient the student and help him know what to expect from the text.

Dialogues

The LISTENING IN dialogues are intended to introduce the grammatical forms and communicative functions in context. They should always be read first by the instructor to model the intonation and the pronunciation. Students may then be asked to read them. The instructor should answer any questions the students might have before going on to the practices. Some dialogues are accompanied by cultural or grammar notes which should be discussed thoroughly.

Practice Exercises

The YOUR TURN exercises which follow the short introductory dialogues are generally intended for *immediate* practice of the forms just presented. The instructor should be sure at this point that the students understand the forms presented and use the exercises for oral practice in groups or individually.

The SUMMING UP exercises at the end of each section are intended to review and reinforce all of the forms studied in the unit. Forms from previous units may also be reviewed in these exercises. The student should first try to do the exercises without referring back to the unit. However, when he is unsure, the student should check the summary charts or go back to look at the information in the unit.

Cartoons

The instructor should be sure that the students know the vocabulary from the cartoons ahead of time. Explaining new words while reading the cartoon really destroys the significance of the cartoon. Students should be able to concentrate on the message of the cartoon, not on the difficult vocabulary. The cartoons should be read aloud by the instructor first and the communicative meaning (the point of the cartoon) should be discussed before making an analysis of the grammar and functions involved.

Intonation

Intonation can strongly affect whether one sounds polite or rude. Students should pay close attention to the intonation the instructor uses and try to practice with native speakers whenever possible.

Role Plays

Role play situations are included at the end of the units, as well as in the Review Section at the back of the book.

The role plays at the end of each section are intended to review the functions taught in that unit and may also include some from previous units. The role plays at the back of the book are intended to review a variety of language functions and are best used after completing the entire book.

Role plays provide students with the opportunity to use the language functions they have been studying in a creative way and they are, therefore, of vital importance. The main emphasis should always be on speaking.

It is fun and challenging to have students change roles and ad lib different parts. Below are some suggestions for utilizing the role plays.

In Class/Groups:

1. Students, working in groups, go through the role play orally, each student taking a part, reviewing and discussing alternatives as they go. The instructor circulates among the groups to answer questions and/or offer assistance.
2. Students form groups, as above, and prepare the role play for presentation to the class. Students in the audience take notes on especially good points or problem areas.
3. Students, in groups, write a script for the role play. The instructor corrects the script and discusses problem areas with the students. The role play may then be performed, preferably without the script.

At Home/Individual:

Students are assigned to work on the role plays as homework. The plays are then corrected by the instructor or discussed in pairs or groups during the next class session.

As A Diagnostic Tool/Groups or Individual:

1. Students may be asked to work in groups and then present the role play orally. The instructor evaluates.
2. Students write out one of the role plays in class as a test.

You may want to ask students to create their own role play situations. These might be based on real life experiences, past or future. (For example, a student may have had difficulty in complaining to his landlord about the leak in his ceiling. Or he may want to request that a telephone be installed in his apartment.)

Students may be asked to record their role plays on tape in a language laboratory or at home. The instructor can then listen to the role play and make notes on good points and/or specific problems. If possible, role plays can also be recorded in the classroom.

Additional Teaching Suggestions

Whenever possible students should be encouraged to take note of how language functions are performed in authentic communicative situations outside of the classroom. They should listen to the language used in a variety of situations: television, radio, songs, movies, and, of course, real conversation.

As was noted earlier, the purpose of this text is to increase the learner's communicative competence and performance. The emphasis is, therefore, on teaching the student the appropriate rules of communication and then on giving him/her the opportunity for oral practice.

The instructor should therefore keep his/her explanations and interventions to a minimum. The students should be very active participants in the classroom activities. As much of the class time as possible should be devoted to student oral practice.

The instructor should try to avoid *reading* from the text. S/he should be familiar with the content of the explanations and explain the various forms and uses to the students in his/her own words. S/he may, of course, point out various items in the text. The book must also be referred to, of course, for the oral practice exercises and other oral activities.

If students are having problems with specific grammatical points, structural exercises may be added.

To the Student: Before You Begin

Go over this introduction very carefully with your teacher. It will help you to understand the purpose of the book.

When learning a new language, especially in a classroom situation, we learn a great deal *about* the language. We learn grammar rules and spelling rules, rules for pronunciation and intonation, rules for punctuation, and much more. However, often we still feel uncomfortable and uncertain when we need to use the new language to communicate. We feel inadequately prepared to say exactly what we want to say, in the way we want to say it.

In order to feel comfortable when speaking a language it is not enough to know only the *grammatical* rules. We must also know the *social* rules. Perhaps you already know English grammar quite well but you may still feel unsure of yourself when speaking to people outside the classroom. You want to be polite but you are not sure what forms and expressions are appropriate in a formal situation and which ones are more suitable to use with classmates and friends. You also want to know which expressions sound impolite. And you may wonder how to decide in the first place when a situation is formal and when it's informal.

Here are some situations which may be familiar to you.

- You want to ask a stranger for directions to the post office. You know how to say, "Where is the post office?" but you're not sure if that's the most polite way to approach a stranger.
- Perhaps you have done something to offend an American friend. You said, "I'm sorry," but your friend still seems angry. Is there something else you should have said?
- Maybe you've asked a professor a question and received a cold answer. Was the professor being rude, or did you ask the question impolitely without knowing it?
- You've been invited to dinner at someone's home and you cannot attend. You want to know how to refuse in a polite way. You're worried about offending the person who invited you.

In the situations mentioned here, and in most situations, there are many different ways to express exactly the same information. Most often there are reasons for the variety of possible forms. One way may be more polite. Another way is very strong and direct. Still a third way may be indirect. The purpose of this book is to help you know which forms are appropriate in which situations.

You will see that often you have a number of choices, especially in informal situations. Imagine that you are talking with your friend during a break and your friend lights up a cigarette. What would you say if you wanted to discourage your friend from smoking? Jot it down here.

Now compare what you wrote with what your classmates wrote. Did you say something similar to the following?

1. Quit smoking.
2. You shouldn't smoke.
3. Why don't you kick the habit?
4. You'd better give up cigarettes.
5. Do you know that smoking is dangerous?
6. If I were you, I'd try to give up cigarettes.
7. Smoking is really bad for your health.

All of these convey the same information but some are more forceful (for example, the first four) while others are less direct and therefore less strong (the final three) but are more polite. (These sentences are given in descending order of directness.)

So you can see that in an informal situation you have several choices. The choice depends on your intention and your relationship with the other person. However, sometimes a choice might be inappropriate. For example, in the situation above you would sound a bit strange if you said:

"I would strongly recommend that you stop smoking."

The grammar is fine but this sentence would be appropriate only in a more formal situation. (Longer sentences tend to be more formal.) Likewise, "Why don't you kick the habit?" (number 3 above) would probably sound quite rude in a formal situation. Sentences 5, 6, and 7 would be "safe," i.e. they would be appropriate in either a formal or an informal situation.

You must also take intonation into consideration, however. The imperative form may sound polite if the tone of the voice is polite whereas "Do you know that smoking is dangerous?" may sound rude when said brusquely.

Every language and culture has its own rules of politeness and appropriateness. Look at the cartoon below from an American newspaper which deals with a social rule of the English language.

In your country, how would you refuse food politely in a situation like this? Compare your answer with your classmates' answers. Discuss any differences.

Perhaps a simple "No" would be appropriate in your country. Perhaps "No, thank you" would be appropriate just as it would be in the United States. Maybe the appropriate response would depend on the relationship of the people involved. In the situation above a granddaughter is talking to her grandmother, but in the United States "No, thank you" would be appropriate in any situation, formal or informal.

This book will help you understand what the different ways of saying things are and how to choose the way that is the most appropriate. Your choice will depend on:

who you are talking to

what your *relationship* to that person is

what the *situation* is

what your *attitude* toward the situation and the person is

NOTES ON "FORMAL" VS. "INFORMAL"

Sometimes Americans seem so informal that it's difficult to be sure how to show respect to people who should be given respect. In the same way, sometimes we're not sure how to be informal with people we become friends with.

In this text you will find many examples of formal and informal ways to say things. Once you have learned the difference between the formal and informal forms, then you must decide when to use them. This can sometimes be confusing. If you are unsure, it is generally better to be too polite or too formal than to be too informal.

In many cultures and languages, the rules for determining how you should speak with other people are very clear. In American culture it is not always as easy to determine when to say something in a formal way and when to say something in an informal way. Here are some general rules to help you.

Formal ways of speaking are generally used when you're speaking with someone who is older than you, especially if you do not know him/her well. Formal language is usual when speaking to someone who is your superior, such as your boss, your teacher or your advisor. With strangers, such as store clerks, bank tellers, office workers or bus drivers, it is generally polite to use more formal speech.

The following chart should be useful. Americans consider themselves as the social equal of others, even while they observe these forms of politeness. It shows the four basic social relationships and gives examples of each.

Speaker — Person Spoken To		**Degree of Formality**
Student	→ Teacher	Usually very formal and very indirect.
Employee	→ Boss	Direct or informal forms may be considered rude and disrespectful.
Student	→ Advisor	
Younger	→ Older	
Patient	→ Doctor	
Teacher	→ Student	Usually formal, but not always.
Advisor	→ Student	Can be very direct, especially when giving directions.
Boss	→ Employee	
Older	→ Younger	
Doctor	→ Patient	
Stranger	↔ Stranger	Generally formal, polite forms.
Teller	↔ Customer	Direct forms may be used in business interactions when the conversation concerns the duties of the business person. However, if the conversation does *not* directly concern business, less direct forms are used.
Waiter	↔ Customer	
Bus Driver	↔ Passenger	
Student	↔ Student	Usually informal.
Friend	↔ Friend	May be very direct, but should also be polite.
Husband	↔ Wife	
Colleague	↔ Colleague	

Formal expressions are generally longer and use more fixed phrases; they are often more tentative and indirect. Informal expressions are usually shorter, more direct, and use fewer fixed phrases; there is usually a much wider choice of appropriate expressions.

Discuss the chart with your classmates and compare the various types of relationships. Consider the following questions:

- What is the relationship between teacher and student in your country?
- What is the relationship between colleagues?
- What is the relationship between a waiter and his customers? etc.

As with most rules, there are exceptions. Student/teacher or boss/employee relationships are not *always* formal. Some people who are in positions of authority prefer an informal relationship. You must begin to notice the clues. A boss or teacher who prefers a formal relationship will often ask to be called by his/her title and last name (e.g. Dr. Jones, Ms. Courtney, Professor Daniels). If a teacher or supervisor or older person says, "Please call me John" or "Please call me Susan," this often signals that he or she would prefer a less formal relationship. However, continue to be polite and respectful.

Usually relationships between people of the same age and status are more informal (fellow students or co-workers), but again there are no firm rules in American culture. Even people of the same age and position may be formal if they do not know each other well.

Also, relationships may change. A formal relationship may become an informal relationship. For example, when you first meet a new neighbor, you may relate to each other on a formal basis. Perhaps, after you've lived near each other for a while, done favors for each other, or socialized, you may become more friendly and less formal.

Certain formal relationships, however, may remain formal even after you have known someone for a long time. For example, your supervisor or teacher may be friendly, but continue to prefer a formal relationship even after he or she has known you for several years.

The situation may also influence the formality of a relationship. You may have a teacher who prefers a formal relationship with his or her students. After the course is over, however, when you no longer have a student/teacher relationship with your ex-teacher, he or she may become more informal.

In this text, when you are asked to do exercises in which you must decide whether to use a formal or informal form, follow these guidelines (unless your teacher or the directions state otherwise):

- Use formal ways of speaking when the exercises say, "boss, teacher, professor, supervisor, advisor, or stranger."
- Use informal ways of speaking when the exercises say, "friend, classmate, co-worker, or family member."

The text will often point out "safe" forms which can be used in most situations.

In this book you will learn how to:

greet people

make introductions

say good-bye

request, command, and refuse

advise, suggest, and caution

promise

apologize

agree and disagree

compliment and congratulate

criticize

complain

Before you begin to study the communicative functions listed above, complete the written exercise below. Write it on a separate sheet of paper. Save this exercise until you have completed the entire book. Then complete the exercise again on a new sheet of paper. Compare your new responses with your old ones.

WRITTEN EXERCISE

Write what you would say in each of the situations below.

Example: You're riding in a car with your friend who is driving much too fast. Tell him/her to slow down.

Could you please slow down? You're making me nervous.

1. Introduce your brother to your English teacher.
2. Greet your classmate before class.
3. Say good-bye to your advisor before you leave for summer vacation.
4. Ask your friend to lend you his/her pen.
5. Tell your next door neighbor to turn down his/her radio. It's 11 p.m. and you want to sleep.
6. Tell your roommate not to wear white shorts to the class picnic. They'll get dirty.
7. Warn your classmate not to skip class tomorrow because there will be a quiz.
8. Tell your friend never to make fun of you again. If he/she does, it will be the end of your friendship.
9. Tell your teacher that you'll try not to be late to class again. You have been late two days in a row.
10. You step on a stranger's toes on the bus. What do you say to him?

While studying this book, you will be given lots of opportunities to speak. When you've finished the book, you will know many communicative rules and your English will be more fluent. These are the two principal goals of this book. At the same time, your grammar will undoubtedly improve as well.

One note of warning. Don't be surprised if your instructor or English-speaking friends sometimes disagree with the book. The way in which we say things is sometimes influenced by where we are from (the East, the South, a big city, a small town, etc.), whether we are male or female, or how old we are.

Enjoy yourself and SAY THE RIGHT THING!

UNIT **I**

GREETING PEOPLE, MAKING INTRODUCTIONS, SAYING GOOD-BYE

Greeting People

Greetings are words of welcome. They are the first words that we say on seeing someone we know. By greeting someone, we acknowledge his or her presence and express respect. We can do this in an informal or a formal way.

INFORMAL GREETINGS

These forms are used in encounters between people who know one another or who share similar positions (e.g. classmates and colleagues). Many of these are exchanges using fixed expressions (that is, words which are always used in the same way.)

For example, if two friends meet they could say:

Tim:	Hi!	Dan:	Hi, Tim!
	How are you? How are you doing? How's it going? How've you been?		Not bad. OK. Fine. All right.
	What's new? What's happening? What's up?		Not much. Nothing much. Nothing special.

"How are you?" usually acts as part of the greeting, rather than a real question. The usual answer is simply "Fine" or "Fine, thanks." However, among friends a more truthful response may be given, and a short explanation may be added.

First names are used in informal situations among family members, friends, classmates, and colleagues.

Notice that any of the responses in a group work with any of the matched greetings.

Listening In

A. Two classmates greet each other in class.

Rita: Hi, Mark! How are you doing?

Mark: Not so good. I've got a bad cold.

Rita: Yeah, a lot of people have colds. It's this crazy weather—cold one minute and hot the next.

The expressions "Hi," "How's it going?" or "How are you doing?" are appropriate only in an informal situation.

B. Two classmates meet after the summer vacation.

Cindy: Hi, Grace! How have you been?

Grace: OK. What's new with you?

Cindy: Nothing special right now. I took a course in Japanese this summer, though. It was fun!

The expression "How have you been?" indicates that you haven't seen the person in a while. This would not be appropriate to say to a person you see daily.

When responding to the question, "What's new?" you may make a brief comment about something you've been doing or are planning to do.

Your Turn

Use informal expressions to complete the following exchanges of greetings and responses. Choose a partner and practice orally first by yourselves. Then present the dialogues in front of the class.

1. Two friends meet on the subway.
2. Two colleagues meet at a party.
3. Two classmates meet after spring vacation.
4. Two neighbors meet at a bus stop.
5. Two friends meet at the supermarket.
6. Two classmates meet in the school parking lot.

Informal greetings are often accompanied by a nod of the head or a slight wave of the hand.

FORMAL GREETINGS

These expressions are used when greeting someone who is older, or to whom we wish to show special respect. They are also used with strangers or with people we don't know very well.

A clerk in a drugstore might greet a customer in this way, and receive these responses:

Clerk:				Customer:
	Hello,	Mr. Mrs. Miss Dr.	Smith.	Hello.
(or)	Good morning, Good afternoon, Good evening,	Mr. Mrs. Miss Dr. sir.	Smith.	Good morning. Good afternoon. Good evening.
(or)	How are you?			Fine, thank you. (and you?)

Formal greetings are often accompanied by a handshake.

When the last name of a person is not known, you may use *sir* for a man.

Titles such as Dr., Mr., Mrs., Ms., or Miss are followed by last names, (Dr. Smith, Mrs. Brown). *Doctor* is sometimes used alone, as is *Professor*.

Listening In

A. In a bank.

Teller: Good morning, sir. How are you?

Customer: Fine, thank you. And you?

Teller: Fine.

Customer: I'd like to deposit this check.

B. In a classroom.

Professor: Hello, Mrs. Brown. How are you?

Mrs. Brown: Good afternoon, Professor Reese. I'm fine, thanks.

Depending on the time of day, *good morning, good afternoon,* or *good evening* may be used as greetings. *Good night* is not used as a greeting; it is used only when saying good-bye at night or when a person is ready to go to bed. *Hello* may be used to replace *good morning, good afternoon,* or *good evening.*

C. In an office.

Secretary: Good morning, Mr. Edwards.

Mr. Edwards: Good morning, Ralph. How are you?

Secretary: Fine, thank you.

An employer may use an employee's first name when addressing him/her. The employee should not use the employer's first name without permission.

Your Turn

A. Use the formal expressions to complete the following exchange of greetings and responses. Choose a partner and practice orally first by yourselves. Then present the dialogues in front of the class.

1. Jenny runs into a friend of her father's downtown.
2. Mrs. Thomas goes into the pharmacy to pick up her weekly prescription. She greets the pharmacist.

It is important to be polite, firm, but not arrogant when speaking with store clerks, waiters, waitresses and other service employees.

B. Look over the following list of situations. Be prepared to greet or respond, using the formal expressions.

1. You happen to meet your biology professor in the school cafeteria at breakfast time.
2. You stop for a snack at a coffee shop and are greeted by the owner.
3. You see your student advisor from last year in the library.

C. Respond to the following greetings in an appropriate way as they are read aloud by the teacher or another student.

1. Good evening, sir.
2. Hello. How are you, Mr. Jones?
3. Hi. How have you been?
4. How's it going?
5. What's up?

SUMMING UP

Appropriate Responses

For each situation below, choose the most appropriate greeting or response. Be prepared to explain the reason for your choice.

Example: You see a friend on the bus. She says, "How's it going?" You respond:

a) Nothing much. (This would be a response to "What's new?")
b) OK. (This would be a very appropriate response.)
c) Good afternoon. (This would be an appropriate response to "Hello," or "Good afternoon." It would be too formal here.)

1. You arrive in class and greet your teacher.
   a) What's up?
   b) Good morning.
   c) How's it going?

2. You pass a man on the street whom you have met only once at a party. He says, "Hello. How are you?" You respond:
   a) Terrible. My wife is angry with me.
   b) Not much.
   c) Fine, thanks. And you?

3. You run into a former classmate. She says, "Hi! How have you been?" You respond:
   a) Not much lately.
   b) Pretty good.
   c) Nothing much.

Making Introductions

We introduce people who don't know each other, and we introduce ourselves to people who don't know us. We can do this in a formal way or in an informal way.

INFORMAL INTRODUCTIONS

These forms are used in situations that do not require a high degree of formality. Such situations usually involve persons in similar positions (e.g. two students, two colleagues). Shaking hands is not always carried out in informal situations but you may shake hands if you like. Do not be offended or insulted if people in the United States do not always shake hands. It is less common between two women or between a man and a woman than between two men. It is also less common than in many other parts of the world.

Let's take a look at a situation in which introductions would be in order. Paul is introducing two classmates, Susan and Greg, who don't know each other.

Paul:	Greg Davis, meet Susan Jackson.	(or)	Greg, this is Susan.	(or)	Greg, I want you to meet Susan.
Greg:	Hi, Susan.		Hello, Susan. Nice meeting you.		Glad to meet you.
Susan:	Hi, Greg.		Nice meeting you, too.		Me, too.

When you are introducing two people, always try to add some information about one or both of them. This will give them some basis for continuing the conversation.

Listening In

Paul: Greg, meet Susan. Sue was in my math class last semester.

Greg: Hello, Susan. Nice meeting you.

Susan: Hi. Glad to meet you, too.

Greg: Are you a math major?

Susan: No, I'm majoring in computer science.

Your Turn

Make informal introductions in the following situations. Note: remember to give *extra* information.

1. Introduce two friends. One is your roommate and the other is a former classmate.
2. Introduce a friend of yours to your brother.
3. Introduce the person on your left to the person sitting on your right.
4. You are having a party. Introduce two people who don't know each other.

We often feel awkward meeting new people because we don't know what to talk to them about. Providing some information when you introduce people can make everyone more comfortable. We usually tell the person's relationship to us as well.

For example:

This is my brother Tom. He lives in Oregon.

This is my father. He's here visiting for a few weeks.

This is my roommate Lucinda. She's on the basketball team.

INFORMAL SELF-INTRODUCTIONS

These forms are used when you are introducing yourself to another person in an informal situation.

Let's look at a possible situation. Rita is introducing herself to a new girl in the dorm.

Rita: Hello. I'm Rita Simon. (or) Hi! My name is Rita Simon.

Carol: My name is Carol Wong. Hi! I'm Carol Wong.

Listening In

Rita: Hi. I'm Rita Simon. I live on this floor.

Carol: Hi, Rita. My name is Carol Wong. Glad to meet you.

Rita: Nice to meet you, too. Why don't you stop by? I'm in Room 209.

Your Turn

Introduce yourself in the following informal situations.

1. Introduce yourself to your new neighbor in your apartment building.
2. Introduce yourself to the person sitting next to you in class.
3. Introduce yourself to a person at your friend's party.
4. Introduce yourself to a new player on your soccer team.
5. Introduce yourself to a new member of your chess club.

FORMAL INTRODUCTIONS

These forms are used in formal situations when a higher degree of formality is required. It is common to shake hands when being introduced in formal situations, especially between two men.

In a typical situation, a student is introducing his academic advisor, Mr. Davis, to his chemistry professor, Professor Kaufman, at a university party. The student, Ron, has several ways he can do this.

Ron: Professor Kaufman, I would like to introduce Mr. Davis. (or) May I introduce Mr. Davis? (or) I would like you to meet Mr. Davis, Professor Kaufman.

Professor Kaufman has a number of possible responses:

How do you do? (or) I'm pleased to meet you. (or) It's nice to meet you. (or) It's a pleasure to meet you.

Mr. Davis can then reply to Professor Kaufman with the same set of responses.

Listening In

A student, his advisor, and his chemistry professor.

Ron: Professor Kaufman, I would like to introduce my academic advisor, Mr. Davis. Professor Kaufman has just come back from teaching in South America.

Professor Kaufman: How do you do, Mr. Davis?

Mr. Davis: It's a pleasure to meet you, Professor Kaufman. Where were you teaching in South America?

Professor Kaufman: At the University of Bogota.

Mr. Davis: One of my senior lab assistants is from Columbia. I'm sure he'd enjoy talking with you.

Many students feel that the expressions "How do you do?" and "How are you?" are equivalent. However, "How do you do?" is not used as a real question, but as a greeting in formal introductions. An answer is not required.

Your Turn

A. Make introductions in the following situations. Use formal forms. First practice with two classmates. Then give the dialogue for the entire class.

1. Introduce your teacher to your wife/husband/cousin.
2. Introduce your advisor to a new student.
3. Introduce your teacher to a friend.

B. Rewrite the Listening In dialogue between Ron, Professor Kaufman and Mr. Davis. Use different forms. Perform it with two classmates.

FORMAL SELF-INTRODUCTIONS

These forms are used when you are introducing yourself to another person in formal situations. It is appropriate to extend your hand when introducing yourself.

Consider the following situation. A new student introduces herself to the chairman of her department at the university. She has made an appointment to see him. She can begin in these ways:

A professor may call a student by his/her first name, but the student will not use the professor's first name unless invited to do so.

Sara:	May I introduce myself? I'm Sara Rogers.	(or)	Let me introduce myself. I'm Sara Rogers.	(or)	My name is Sara Rogers.
Dr. Haskel:	How are you, Miss Rogers?	(or)	How do you do, Miss Rogers? (Sara)	(or)	It's a pleasure to meet you. (Sara)

Listening In

Here is the student introducing herself:

Sara: Dr. Haskel, may I introduce myself? I'm Sara Rogers. I've just been accepted for the master's program in your department.

Dr. Haskel: How are you, Miss Rogers? Welcome to the university. What can I do for you?

Sara: I need to arrange my schedule for this semester.

Your Turn

Make self-introductions in the following formal situations.

1. Introduce yourself to the manager of your apartment building. You have just moved in with your sister and you haven't met the manager yet.
2. Introduce yourself to the foreign student advisor's secretary. Ask to make an appointment with the foreign student advisor.
3. Introduce yourself to the foreign student advisor.

SUMMING UP: INTRODUCTIONS

Listening In

Read this dialogue. Identify the different types of introductions. Which ones are formal? Which ones are informal? Are there any examples of self-introductions?

Louise: Hi. I'm Louise Smith. I've seen you in my math class, haven't I?

Jim: Right. My name is Jim Robinson. Glad to meet you, Louise. (turning to the friend who is with him) Hey, Bob! This is Louise Smith. She's in our math class.

Bob: Hi, Louise. How are you doing?

Louise: Fine. Nice to meet you. Isn't that Professor Aronson over there? I've never met him, but I'm interested in taking his class next term.

Jim: Come on. I'll introduce you to him. (Walking to the table where Professor Aronson is sitting)

Excuse me, Professor Aronson. I would like to introduce Louise Smith. She's hoping to register for your class next term.

Professor A: It's a pleasure to meet you, Miss Smith.

Louise: How do you do, Professor Aronson? I'm looking forward to the class. Everyone says it's great.

Your Turn

A. Divide into groups of two or three to prepare the following role plays. (The number of characters needed is in parentheses.) Make the introduction and then continue a short conversation.

1. Introduce your father to your American roommate. (3)
2. Introduce your best friend (an American) to your mother. (3)
3. Introduce yourself to a woman/man you would like to meet at a party. (2)
4. Introduce yourself to the manager of an office where you would like to work. (2)

B. Complete the exchange below.

Bill: Hi, I'm Bill Reid. I'm a friend of your brother's.

Lee: ______________________________

Bill: ______________________________

Lee: ______________________________

Appropriate Responses

Discuss the following introductions and explain why you feel that your response is the most appropriate. Be prepared to explain why the other responses are equally appropriate or less appropriate.

For example:

You are introducing a close friend to another classmate in the cafeteria.

a) Mr. Lee, I would like you to meet Richard Goldberg. (too formal)
b) Dave Lee, this is Richard Goldberg. (appropriate)
c) Dave, may I introduce you to Richard Goldberg? (too formal)

1. You have just been introduced to your new psychology professor.
   a) Hi. How are you doing?
   b) How do you do?
   c) Hello. How's it going?
2. You have just been introduced to your roommate's friend at a party.
   a) Nice to meet you.
   b) It's a pleasure to meet you.
   c) How have you been?

Role Play

Characters: Miguel Sanchez
Sam Potter
Professor Martin
George Wilson

Miguel and Sam arrive at the concert hall and take their seats. Miguel notices some familiar faces around him. Seated in front of him is his math teacher, Professor Martin. He *greets* him and then *introduces* him to Sam. Seated behind Miguel is George, a close friend of his from class who has just returned from spending his summer vacation in Greece. Miguel *greets* George and then he *introduces* him to Sam. Then the concert begins.

Think about these questions before you begin.

1. How well does Miguel know George?
2. Is he on the same level of formality with Professor Martin as he is with George?

(See the preface for suggestions on various ways to use the Role Plays.)

Saying Good-Bye

We say good-bye to people when we are leaving them or when they are leaving us. We may use formal or informal expressions.

For example, after being introduced to your friend's brother:	Nice meeting you. See you later.
but after meeting your instructor:	It was a pleasure meeting you. Good-bye.
When you leave your friends you can say:	Bye. See you around.
but if you are leaving people you do not know that well:	Good-bye.

In the dialogue, Bob uses the expression, "I've got to go." Similar expressions are:

I've got to run.
I've got to hurry.
I'd better go.
I should be going.
It's getting late.

"You, too" is an abbreviated form of "It was nice meeting you, too."

Expressions such as "See you later" and "See you around" are used if we'll be seeing the person again soon. Similar expressions are:

See you in class.
See you next week, etc.
See you soon.

Expressions which can be used in place of "So long" are:

Bye.
Good-bye.
Take it easy.
Take care.
Have a good day.

After class or a meeting we can often make our partings very brief by using one of the expressions above. But when we have been conversing with someone alone or in a small group, it is considered polite to justify our leaving. We might say:

I must leave because I've got to catch my bus.

I have to go because I'm meeting a friend for dinner.

I've got to run because it's late.

INFORMAL GOOD-BYE FOLLOWING INTRODUCTION

These forms are used when parting from someone after an informal introduction.

Listening In

Two classmates have just met for the first time and are ending their conversation.

Bob: Well, I've got to go. I have a class at nine. Nice meeting you.

Ted: You, too. See you later.

Bob: Yeah. See you around.

INFORMAL GOOD-BYE WITH FRIENDS

Listening In

Two roommates are getting ready to leave the house in the morning.

Jeff: It's already nine. I've got to run.
Brad: Me, too. See you tonight.
Jeff: So long.

Your Turn

A. Substitute similar expressions for the underlined parts in dialogue above. Practice orally with a partner.

B. Complete the following parting phrases. You are saying good-bye to your friend after class. Do this exercise orally. There are several different ways to complete each one.

1. See you ______
2. I have to ______
3. I really should ______

4. I must _______ because _______
5. Take _______
6. I'd better _______

Role play

Choose one of the situations below and practice it with a partner. Perform it for the class. Use at least six exchanges.

1. Two friends are saying good-bye after meeting at a party.
2. Two classmates are saying good-bye at the end of the semester.
3. Two neighbors are saying good-bye because one is moving to another state.

FORMAL GOOD-BYE FOLLOWING INTRODUCTION

These forms are used when saying good-bye to a person that we have just met formally.

Listening In

Nancy Chen has gone to Professor Goodman's office to introduce herself. She will be taking one of his courses this semester.

Nancy: I know you're very busy, Professor Goodman. I don't want to take up any more of your time. It was a pleasure meeting you.

Professor Goodman: My pleasure, Miss Chen. I hope we'll have the chance to talk again sometime soon. Have a nice day.

Nancy: Thank you. You, too. Good-bye.

Professor Goodman: Good-bye.

Parting is very often more complex than greeting. When parting it is common to express several things: an excuse for leaving (e.g. "I don't want to take up any more of your time"), thanks (e.g. "Thank you"), a wish ("Have a nice day"), and a final statement (e.g. "I hope we'll have a chance to talk again sometime soon").

The word *good-bye* is most often the last thing we say when parting.

Note that Nancy apologizes for taking up the professor's time. That is extremely polite but not necessary.

FORMAL GOOD-BYE WITH ACQUAINTANCES

These forms are used in more formal situations in which the speakers have previously met.

Listening In

A. A student is talking to his academic advisor.

David: I really should leave for class now. Thank you very much for your help, Mrs. Williams.

Mrs. Williams: You're welcome, David. Have a good semester. Don't hesitate to drop in when you have any questions.

David: I won't. Good-bye.

Mrs. Williams: Good-bye.

When making an excuse to leave or to end a conversation, these modals are most frequently used: I *must* go, I *should* go, I *have to* go. These expressions indicate that the person regrets that the conversation cannot continue.

It would be considered impolite to end the conversation by saying: I want to leave, I'm going, I will leave.

B. A student is having a conference with the teacher.

Liz: Yes, I understand it now, Professor Sears.

Professor Sears: Good. If you have any more questions in the future, be sure to come and see me.

Liz: I will. Thank you very much.

Professor Sears: That's all right. Good-bye.

The visitor or the person detaining someone else should be sensitive to cues that the other person wants to end the conversation. In this dialogue, Professor Sears makes it clear that it is time for the student to leave. He might also have said:

I'm glad you stopped by.
I'm pleased I was able to help you.

- How would you show that a conversation was over in your culture?
- How do you say good-bye to your teacher, your best friend and your neighbors?

C. A student meets one of her former teachers in the bookstore. After they chat a while, they say good-bye.

Rebecca: It was nice seeing you again, Mrs. Rhodes. I hope to see you again soon.

Notice that if you have just met the person for the first time (i.e. after an introduction), you say:

It was nice *meeting* you.

If, on the other hand, you already know the person and run into him/her somewhere, you say:

It was nice *seeing* you.

Mrs. Rhodes: I hope so, too. Have a good day.

Rebecca: The same to you. Good-bye.

Mrs. Rhodes: Bye.

In response to the expression "Have a good (or nice) day," you can say:

The same to you.
You, too.
Likewise.
You have a good day, too.

Your Turn

Prepare dialogues in which two people are concluding a conversation. Use expressions from the preceding dialogues.

1. A student is talking to an academic advisor.
2. A student is talking to a professor in front of the library.
3. A young man is talking to his girlfriend's father.
4. A young woman is talking to her roommate's aunt.
5. An employer is talking to a clerk.
6. A woman is talking to her supervisor.

SUMMING UP: SAYING GOOD-BYE

Appropriate Responses

Discuss the appropriateness of the following responses.

1. You are saying good-bye to a woman you have just met in the cafeteria.
   a) Good morning.
   b) Nice meeting you.
   c) Nice seeing you again.
2. You run into an old friend on the street whom you haven't seen for a year. The last thing you say to her is:
   a) Nice meeting you.
   b) How have you been?
   c) Nice seeing you.

3. You are saying good-bye to a colleague who is leaving for a new job abroad.
   a) See you around.
   b) Have a good day.
   c) Keep in touch. Good-bye.

SUMMING UP: GREETING PEOPLE, INTRODUCING, SAYING GOOD-BYE

Role Play

Characters: Lorraine Fleming
Clyde Fleming, her husband
Maryanne Choi
Mr. Richards, the boss
Mrs. Richards, his wife

Lorraine works part-time at the library. Her friend and colleague Maryanne is preparing to leave her present job in order to take a new position abroad. There is a farewell party at the library this evening. When Lorraine arrives at the party, she first *greets* her boss, Mr. Richards, who has just returned from a month's vacation. Her boss then *introduces* Lorraine to his wife. Lorraine's husband walks over to the three of them and *introduces* himself. Mrs. Richards whispers something into her husband's ear and he then *makes an excuse for leaving* the party so early. They *say good-bye* to some of the guests. Lorraine decides that it's time for her to leave also, so she finds Maryanne to *say good-bye.* Lorraine and her husband leave shortly after Mr. and Mrs. Richards.

Prepare this role play and present it to your class. More characters (guests) may be added, if desired.

Think about these questions before beginning your preparation.

1. Is it polite to whisper in someone's ear when others are present?
2. How can you justify Mrs. Richards' behavior? What do you think she said?
3. How do *you* know when to leave a party?
4. Why do you think Lorraine and her husband left the party early?

Summary Chart: Greeting People

Type	*Sample sentence*	*Sample response*	*Notes*
Informal	Hi, Jane.	Hi.	First names are used in most cases.
	How are you?	Fine. (or truthful response)	A truthful response (if you are *not* fine) is more likely in informal situations. In this case, a brief explanation is usually offered. (In response to the greeting "How are you doing?", you may answer "Terrible. I've had a headache all morning.")
	How are you doing? How's it going? How have you been?	O.K. Not bad. All right.	
	What's new? What's happening? What's up?	Not much. Nothing much. Nothing special.	
Formal	Hello, Mr. Johnson. Hello.	Hello. Good morning/ afternoon/evening.	First names are not used with titles except in rare instances.
	Hello, Mrs. Smith/ Miss Smith.		Notice that titles used with last names differ from those used alone, with the exception of Dr. (doctor) or Professor which can be used with or without the last name.
	Hello, Dr. Richards. Hello, Doctor.		
	Good morning, Mr. Johnson Good afternoon, Mrs. Smith Good evening, Dr. Richards.		*Hello* is used at any time of the day or night. Remember that *Good night* is not a greeting.
	How are you?	Fine, thank you. (And you?) Very well, thank you. (And you?)	A truthful response (if you are not fine) is usually avoided. Handshakes are acceptable, but not necessary.

Summary Chart: Making Introductions

Type	*Sample sentence*	*Sample response*	*Notes*
Informal	Rita, this is Jim Gray. He's a classmate. Jim, this is Rita Hanson. Rita, meet Jim. He's a classmate.	Hi. Hello. Nice to meet you/ Glad to meet you. How are you doing? How are you?	Use first and last name or first name only. Add information about the person being introduced. Handshaking not necessary.
Informal/ Self	Hi. I'm Dave Parker. I live in the apartment next to yours. Hi. My name's Rick. I'm in your chemistry class.	Same responses as above (informal).	Handshaking not necessary. Add appropriate information about yourself.
Formal	Mr. Smith, I would like to introduce you to Phil Harvey. He's the new member. Phil, this is John Smith. Mr. Smith, may I introduce you to Mr. Harvey. He's the new member.	It's a pleasure to meet you. Pleased to meet you. How do you do? How are you?	Use title + last name, or first name + last name. No answer is necessary with "How do you do?" Handshaking is common.
Formal/ Self	May I introduce myself. I'm . . . . Let me introduce myself. My name is	Same responses as above (formal).	May extend hand for handshake. Use first name + last name. Identify yourself further.

Summary Chart: Saying Good-Bye

Type	*Sample sentence*	*Sample response*	*Notes*
Informal/ follow introductions	Nice meeting you.	You, too.	
Informal/ acquaintances	I've got to (go/leave/ hurry/run.) Have a nice/good day (week/time, etc.) Bye/So long/See you/Good-bye. Take it easy/Take care.	 You, too.	
Formal/ follow introductions	It was nice meeting you. It was a pleasure meeting you.	My pleasure. It was nice meeting you, too.	Do not confuse "It was nice *seeing* you." with "It was nice *meeting* you."
Formal/ acquaintances	I have to (leave/go). I must (leave/go). I should (leave/go). It was nice seeing you. It was nice to see you. Have a good day/etc. Good-bye (Good night)	Certainly. Of course. The same to you.	Remember that good night is used for saying good-bye at night.

UNIT 

COMMANDING AND REQUESTING, REFUSING

Commanding and Requesting

We give commands and make requests when we want someone to do something or not to do something. A command is an order and is therefore stronger; we are telling someone what to do. A request is less strong; we are asking someone to do something, or asking if *we* can do something.

As we make a command more polite it may take the same form as a request, and the degree of politeness may depend on intonation. Here are examples, beginning with the strongest command and ending with the most polite request.

Come here.	I need your help.	You'd better study.	Would you help me?	I wonder if I could use your pen.
(Imperative)	(Statement)	(Strong Modals)	(Direct Question)	(Indirect Question)

IMPERATIVE

The imperative is the most common form for commands. It is very direct and the speaker usually expects immediate results. This form is used in informal situations among friends or persons in similar positions such as classmates or colleagues. It is *not* used with someone in a position of authority.

Listening In

A negative imperative form is used to tell someone *not* to do something. Juan could say, "Don't crack your gum."

A. Two students are watching television together.

Juan: Stop cracking your gum! It's driving me crazy.

Gary: Sorry.

Because commands are very direct and strong, they are often made more polite by adding "please." Even with the addition of "please," commands should not be used to persons in positions of authority. Listen to the teacher's intonation, as imperatives with "please" may be either commands or requests.

Other examples with "please":

Please stop cracking your gum.
Get me one, too, please.

B. Two friends are eating in a fast-food restaurant.

Kathy: Oh, I forgot to get a straw. Be back in a minute.

Martin: Get me one, too.

Kathy: OK.

C. In a school cafeteria.

Harry: Pass the salt, please.

Donna: Here you are.

D. In a restaurant.

Waiter: Will that be all?

Customer: Bring the check, please.

Waiter: Certainly.

Imperatives are commonly used to give directions. In this case, they are not considered impolite.

E. The professor is giving the class an assignment.

Professor: For tomorrow, read pages 24–56 and write out the exercises at the end of Chapter Five on page 57. Please think carefully before you answer the questions.

Student: Will you collect the exercises?

Professor: No, but bring them to class. We'll go over them together.

- Notice how the professor uses imperatives for giving directions. Find the imperatives.

F. Two roommates are talking.

Roger: I'm going to study in the library for a few hours.

Walt: When will you be back?

Roger: Around 10:30. If anybody calls, take a message, would you?

Walt: Sure. See you later.

- Find the imperatives.

A question tag is often added to an affirmative imperative to make it sound more polite. This changes a direct command into an indirect command by adding an interrogative form. This form, however, is still too strong to use with persons in positions of authority. We can add:

. . . , could you?
. . . , will you?
. . . , would you?

Your Turn

A. Complete the following dialogues by using an appropriate imperative verb form. Use the verb given in parentheses. Add "please" or a question tag, if appropriate.

1. Peter, a friend of Nancy's, is admiring some art objects in her home.

   Peter: What's this?

   Nancy: Can't you tell? It's a glass elephant. Mary gave it to me for my birthday.

   (Peter reaches over to pick it up.)

   Nancy: (touch) ______________ . It's very fragile.

   Peter: Oh, I'm sorry.

2. In a chemistry lab.

   Instructor: We are going to do some experiments with helium today. First, (put on) ______________ your lab coats.

   Ellen: Oh, I left mine at home!

   Instructor: (wear) ______________ Claudia's. She's absent today.

Certain imperative forms are commonly used to give commands. These forms, however, are considered very friendly and polite and may be used by anyone. Invitations are often given in this way. These fixed expressions are polite because you are telling someone to do something which is positive.

Stop by sometime.
Come visit us sometime.
Say hello to your family for me.
Give me a call.
Don't forget to write.
Call me sometime.
Have a good day.
Have a nice day/vacation/weekend.

B. Read the following situations. Then give an appropriate command using an imperative verb form. Discuss your reasons for choosing the form.

1. Your friend's five-year-old son is pounding on your piano. You are trying to have a conversation with your friend. Tell the child to be quiet.
2. You want your classmate to return your book. He keeps forgetting to give it back. Tell him to bring it tomorrow.
3. Your friend keeps blowing cigarette smoke in your face. Tell him to stop it.
4. You want your friend to come and visit you sometime.
5. Tell your classmate to call you this evening to discuss the history assignment.

STATEMENT

We can also use declarative sentences for commands. These would not generally be used when speaking to a person in authority. Some common expressions are:

I want	I want you to	I need	I would like	I would like you to . . . .

(These two are the most polite forms.)

Listening In

A. A teacher is talking to a student.

Teacher: I want you to redo this exercise. There are a lot of mistakes.

Student: All right. I'll try to correct them.

B. A lawyer and a secretary.

Lawyer: I would like you to have these papers typed by 3 o'clock. They have to be mailed out today.

Secretary: I'll work on it right away.

Your Turn

Rephrase each of the following using a declarative form.

1. Parent to child: Clean your room.
2. Restaurant customer to waiter: Bring me some ice cream for dessert.
3. Bank customer to teller: Give me a roll of dimes.
4. Drugstore customer to druggist: Give me a bottle of aspirin, please.

STRONG MODALS

The strong modals (should, ought to, had better, must, have to) are commonly used for giving commands. Like imperatives, they are quite forceful, especially *must, had better,* and *have to*. They are generally used between friends or persons in similar positions. They are usually not addressed to persons in positions of authority.

Listening In

A. A teacher is talking to a student during a test. Locate the commands.

Teacher: Sally, you should not talk during a test.

Sally: I'm sorry. I needed an eraser.

Teacher: Well, when you have a problem, you had better ask me, not another student.

B. A professor is upset with one of her students. She has a talk with this student after class. Find the commands given by the professor.

Professor: You must come to class prepared to do the experiments.

John: I'm sorry, but my relatives were here visiting me and I didn't have time to prepare for class.

Professor: This isn't the first time this has happened. You had better make more of an effort to complete the outside work. Students who are not prepared slow the whole class down. I won't tolerate this. It's not fair to those who work hard.

The speakers used declarative statements to phrase their requests. These statements could have been put in the imperative form:

I want you to redo this exercise.
Redo this exercise.

I would like you to have these papers typed . . . .
Type these papers.

In Unit III you will see how many of these forms are also used to give advice. Listen to the teacher's intonation; commands are given more forcefully than advice.

Your Turn

A. Complete the following dialogues using strong modals (should, ought to, must, have to, or had better).

1. A student has come to class late.

   Jill: I'm sorry I was late again today.
   Professor Ortega: ____________.
   Jill: I know. I'll try harder from now on.

2. Two classmates are talking.

   Jim: I forgot to buy some notebook paper. Could you give me some?
   Al: (buy) ____________ .
   Jim: I know, but I forgot. Just give me a couple of pieces, would you?

B. Use strong modals to tell someone to do something.

1. It is your roommate's turn to clean the apartment. He/she is feeling lazy today, but you are having guests later on.
2. One of your classmates keeps talking to the student at the next desk and it's bothering you because you can't hear the instructor.

DIRECT QUESTION

Direct questions are polite commands or requests; they are made still more polite with the addition of "please."

It is always more polite to *ask* someone to do something rather than to *tell* someone to do something. Therefore, interrogative forms are polite in any situation and are always best to use with someone in authority. The following forms are used:

Will you . . . ? — Will you lend me your platter for my party?
Would you . . . ? — Would you hand me that book, please?
Would you mind . . . ? — Would you mind giving me a lift to the meeting?
Can you . . . ? — Can you give that report to me by tomorrow?
Could you . . . ? — Could you please call Jennifer for me tonight?

Listening In

A. A student is meeting with his advisor.

Carl: Would you please help me arrange my schedule for next semester?

Dr. Chen: Of course. What are your plans?

Carl: I want to take only two courses because I have a part-time job. I'm working in the school library.

Dr. Chen: Fine. Will you fill out these forms first, and then we'll discuss your schedule?

When a person uses an interrogative form with a person under his authority, even if he appears to be *asking*, he is actually *telling* the person in the lower position to do something.

B. The instructor is talking to the class.

Mrs. Baylor: Will you please divide into groups of three and prepare the dialogues using the idioms from today's lesson?

Maria: Do you want us to write the dialogues out first?

Mrs. Baylor: Yes. I want you to write the entire text on a sheet of paper and hand it in at the end of class.

- Discuss the forms which Dr. Chen and Mrs. Baylor use. Which do you think are requests, and which do you think are actually commands?

C. Jim is attending a party at Susan's house.

Jim: Would you mind pouring me some coffee?

Susan: Sure. Here you are./No, I don't mind. Here you are.

OR

Jim: Would you pour me some coffee?

Susan: Sure.

In the expressions "Would you mind . . ." and "Do you mind . . . ," "mind" means "object to." The answer can sometimes be confusing. With questions beginning with these expressions, it is always best to give a longer answer to avoid confusion. Study these dialogues carefully. Note the difference between "Would you . . ." and "Would you mind . . ."

A negative response is usually given when the person does not mind. Sometimes the answer, however, is a simple "sure" or "OK."

Notice the verb forms which follow:

Would you pour me some coffee? (simple form of the verb)

Would you mind pouring me some coffee? (-ing form)

We can also use these forms to ask permission to do something ourselves. Instead of saying, "May I . . . ?" or "Can I . . . ?" we can say "Would you mind if I . . . ?" or "Do you mind if I . . . ?"

D. Carol is visiting Leslie's new apartment.

Carol: Would you open the window?

Leslie: OK. Sure. I'd be happy to.

OR

Carol: Would you mind opening the window?

Leslie: No, I'd be happy to.

Your Turn

Change each request for someone to do something to a request for permission to do it yourself.

Notice the verb forms which follow requests for permission using "mind."

Would you mind if I *borrowed* this book? (past form)

Do you mind if I *borrow* this book? (present form)

Note that while both forms are polite, "Would you mind" is more polite.

Examples: Would you mind closing the window?
Would you mind if I closed the window?

Do you mind answering this letter?
Do you mind if I answer this letter?

1. Would you mind turning off the air-conditioning?
2. Would you mind leaving early today?
3. Would you mind stopping at the store?
4. Do you mind cooking chicken for dinner?
5. Do you mind sitting here?

INDIRECT QUESTION

One final way of politely asking someone to do something is by changing a direct question to an indirect question with "I wonder if . . . ." This is a very polite form.

Could you open the door?	I wonder if you could open the door.
Would you give me that pen?	I wonder if you would give me that pen.

Listening In

A. In the classroom.

Student: I wonder if you could explain that problem again.

Teacher: Certainly.

B. At the airport.

Elderly gentleman: I wonder if you would help me get a taxi.

Fellow passenger: I'd be glad to help.

SUMMING UP: COMMANDING AND REQUESTING

Listening In

A. Two students are talking:

Bob: Would you mind if I borrowed your notes to study for the quiz?

Pete: My notes?

Bob: Yeah. I was absent twice this week. Do you mind if I copy yours?

Pete: No, but I can't let you have them overnight. I need them to study, too.

Bob: Well, could I have them for half an hour to make a photocopy?

Pete: Sure. I'll wait for you in the student center. Bring them to me when you're done.

- How many commands and requests can you find in this dialogue? Which are direct? Are they polite or impolite?

Remember that there are several ways to make commands and requests more polite. "Please" can be added to all of these ways.

For example: Give me that pencil.

1. Imperative plus "please." (This is still informal and not appropriate when speaking to a person in authority.)

   Please give me that pencil.

2. Imperative plus tag question. (still informal.)

   Give me that pencil, would you (please)?

3. Question.

   Will you (please) give me that pencil? (more polite)

4. Indirect question.

   I wonder if you could (please) give me that pencil.
   (most polite)

B. In an elevator.

Woman: Excuse me, sir, could you please hold the door open a minute while I get my other suitcase?

Stranger: Certainly. Let me help you. That looks heavy.

Woman: Thanks. I appreciate it. Do you mind pressing "5"; my hands are full.

Stranger: No problem.

Woman: Here's my floor. Thank you so much. Have a nice day.

Stranger: You, too.

- Point out the requests and commands in this dialogue.
- Are all the requests and commands polite?

Your Turn

A. Make each command more polite. Discuss the different ways to do this.

Example: Shut the door.
Please shut the door.
Shut the door, would you please?
Would you please shut the door?
Would you mind shutting the door?
I wonder if you could shut the door?

1. Don't touch the paintings.
2. Bring some wine.
3. Buy some eggs when you go to the store.
4. Be quiet.
5. Don't smoke here.

B. Change each sentence to an interrogative with "would." Be careful. Some are requests for permission and some are not.

Example: Give me a ride to the airport.
Would you mind giving me a ride to the airport?

1. May I borrow your pen?
2. Give me that book.
3. Can I use your car?
4. May I turn in my paper late?
5. Pass me the butter.
6. Correct these homework exercises.

Hw.

Appropriate Responses

A. In each situation, decide which answer(s) are most appropriate. There may be more than one appropriate choice. Discuss your choice(s).

1. You are lost in a strange part of town. You approach a stranger and say:
   a) Tell me where the subway is.
   b) Could you please tell me where the subway is?
   c) Tell me where the subway is, will you?
   d) I wonder if you could please tell me where the subway is.

2. Two students are in the library. One student's pen falls off the table and rolls under his friend's chair. The first student says:
   a) Would you mind handing me that pen?
   b) Hand me my pen, would you?
   c) You have to hand me my pen.
   d) Please hand me my pen.
   e) You ought to hand me my pen.

B. Make each of the following commands or requests more appropriate to the situation. Then rewrite the entire dialogue.

Example: A student believes that her teacher has made a mistake in correcting her test. She asks the teacher to check it again.

Marie: Add up my points again.
Teacher: What?
Marie: You made a mistake in the correction.

This dialogue can be made more polite and appropriate:

Marie: I wonder if you could add up my points again.
Teacher: Oh. Is there a problem?
Marie: I think perhaps there's a mistake.

Notice how impolite the student was in this dialogue because a command was used to the teacher. It was also impolite because the teacher was directly criticized. (You will study more about criticizing in Unit VI.)

C. Make these dialogues more polite. Discuss the different ways to do this.

1. Passenger: Give me change for a dollar.
   Stranger: I don't have it.
2. Customer: Cash this check.
   Teller: I need to see your identification.
3. Classmate A: Type this letter for me.
   Classmate B: I'm busy.
4. Passenger: Change me to a later flight.
   Travel Agent: I'm sorry but all the flights are booked.
5. Student A: Let me use the copy machine before you. I'm in a hurry.
   Student B: No. I was here first. Wait your turn.

What's Happening?

ya = you
bother = disturb

Read the following comic strip and then answer the questions which follow.

1. Was the bird making the requests polite?
2. How many request forms did he use?
3. Why was the other bird so angry? Would you have been angry in this situation?

Your Turn

For each situation, use as many different forms as are appropriate. Discuss your reasons for choosing or not choosing different forms. This exercise may be completed in pairs, in small groups, or in the class as a whole.

1. Ask your professor to spell a difficult word for you.
2. Tell your friend to call you this evening.
3. Ask your roommate to set the alarm clock for 7:00 a.m.
4. Ask your roommate to bring you a cup of coffee when he/she comes back.
5. Tell the bus driver to give you a transfer.
6. Tell the store clerk to give you change for a dollar.
7. Ask your advisor to sign your registration card.
8. Ask your friend to lend you $5.00.

Role Play

Characters: Florence
Gary
Joyce
Matt

Florence is planning a surprise party for her friend Nancy. She *invites* some friends. She *wants* Joyce to help her clean the recreation room and to bake some things. Joyce *asks* Matt and Gary to do some shopping. She *asks* them to buy some soft drinks but *tells* them not to buy any alcoholic drinks. Matt *asks* Gary if he can bring some chairs. Joyce *tells* everyone not to breathe a word to Nancy. Gary *asks* everyone to bring a small gift for Nancy. Florence *insists* that they be at her house by 7:30 p.m. Nancy will be arriving around 8. They complete the plans for the party.

Try to use as many requests and commands as possible in preparing this role play. Try to vary the forms as much as you can. Add additional conversation so that your performance lasts at least ten minutes.

Refusing

When we are asked or ordered to do something, we sometimes refuse, that is, we say no. Perhaps we don't *want* to do what we've been asked to do or perhaps we *can't* do it. When we refuse, we usually give a reason or an excuse for our refusal, otherwise the refusal may be heard as impolite.

Let's look at the following situation. Carl wants Sarah to lend him her lecture notes from the history class. Sarah might say:

No, you're always cutting class and it's just not fair.	(Statement + reason)
I'm sorry, but I left them at home today.	(I'm sorry, + excuse)
I would but I need them myself to study.	(Conditional + excuse)

STATEMENT

Listening In

A. Two roommates are talking.

Joel: It's your turn to clean the room.

Mac: No, it's not my turn and I won't do it.

Joel: OK, I guess it is my turn but I've got to go to the library to study.

Mac: You're always trying to get out of cleaning up. The answer is no.

- What is the relationship between Joel and Mac?
- Why does Mac refuse Joel's request?

Mac's response is very direct and very forceful. This type of response would be used only between equals.

B. Two classmates are talking.

Pamela: Can you lend me a pen?

Denise: No, I've only got one.

Pamela: OK. I'll ask Jerry.

- Do you think that Denise is polite?
- How did Pam react to Denise's refusal?
- Would the form of Denise's refusal have been different if Pamela had been a professor rather than a student?

Denise's response is direct but not as forceful as Mac's. Notice also that Denise explains why she can't do what Pamela requested while Mac emphasizes why he doesn't *want* to do it instead of why he *can't* do it.

Your Turn

Complete the following dialogues using a statement form of refusal.

1. Your friend: Will you help me with my math assignment this afternoon?
   You: No, ______________________________.
2. Your classmate: Can you give me a ride home after class today?
   You: No, ______________________________.
3. Your roommate: Lend me $5.00, will you?
   You: No, ______________________________.

I'M SORRY + EXCUSE

Listening In

Students may enjoy comparing the professor-student relationship in their country and in the U.S.

A potluck supper is a party to which each of the guests brings a portion of the meal. Students may have similar customs in their countries.

The expression "It's too bad" means "It's unfortunate."

A. A professor is inviting his class to his home for a party.

Professor Stafford: I would like all of you to come to my house on Friday night for a potluck supper.

Gail: I'm sorry, Professor Stafford, but I'm going away for the week-end.

Professor Stafford: It's too bad that you have a conflict, Gail. Will anyone else be unable to come?

1. Do you think Gail should have changed her plans so that she could have gone to her professor's party?
2. Have you ever had to refuse a similar invitation? How did you feel?

B. Two students who are strangers meet at a bus stop.

Sam: How much is the fare to Springfield?

Gilbert: 60 cents.

Sam: Can you change a dollar?
Gilbert: I'm sorry. I don't have any change.
Sam: That's OK. I'll ask someone else.

- Do you need exact change for buses in your country?
- Was it proper of Sam to ask a stranger for change?

Your Turn

Complete the following dialogues using "I'm sorry but . . . ."

1. Professor: May I have your assignment?
   You: I'm sorry but ______________________________.
2. Student in the cafeteria: Is it OK if I look at your newspaper?
   You: I'm sorry but ______________________________.
3. Friend: Can you come to my party on Saturday night?
   You: I'm sorry but ______________________________.

CONDITIONAL

Listening In

A. Two classmates meet in the university gym.

Camilla: Why don't you come to the pool with me?
Patrick: I'd like to but I've got to practice basketball now.
Camilla: Well, how about after practice? I'll be there all afternoon.
Patrick: Great! See you then.

- Should Camilla have invited Patrick to go swimming with her?
- Would this have happened in your country?

If Patrick had only answered, "No," that would possibly be understood as a more blunt refusal; that might mean he does not ever want to go.

B. Two students are talking after their afternoon class on Friday.

Richard: Hey, Susan! Do you want to have a drink with me at the Town Inn?
Susan: I would but I have to meet my boyfriend in about ten minutes.
Richard: Well, maybe another time. Have a good weekend.
Susan: You, too. Bye.

- Was Richard's invitation proper?
- Should Susan have accepted?
- Who would have paid for the drinks if Susan had accepted?
- Who would have paid for the drinks in your country?

Your Turn

Complete the following dialogues using a conditional.

1. Classmate: Let's study for the exam together.
   You: I would ____.
2. Professor: Could you lend me a book on your country—in English?
   You: I would ____.

SUMMING UP: REFUSING

Role Play

Choose a partner and act out the following situations. Every request should be refused Use one of the three types of refusals.

1. Your roommate wants to wear your new shoes to the Winter Dance.
2. Your friend wants to borrow your car to go to the supermarket.
3. Your advisor wants to see you a few days after your last examination.
4. A stranger asks if he/she can share a taxi with you.

Summary Chart: Commanding and Requesting

Type	*Sample sentences*	*Notes*
Imperative	Be quiet.	Command; strong and direct. Do not use with persons in authority except in rare instances (e.g., in an emergency. "Don't touch that wire!" See Unit III).
	Be quiet, please. Be quiet, will you?/would you?/ could you?	Adding a question tag or "please" makes it more polite, but still direct.
Statement	I want a cup of coffee. I want you to bring me a cup of coffee.	Command. Very strong and direct.
	I need this letter typed by 10:00.	May be considered impolite, unless it is clearly the person's job to fulfill the speaker's order.
	I would like a cup of coffee, please. I'd like you to bring me a cup of coffee.	"would" makes the command more polite.
Strong Modals	You should be quiet. ought to have to must had better	Command, strong. Never used to persons in authority, unless giving advice which was asked for (See Unit III). Modals are always followed by the simple form of the verb (infinitive without "to").

Summary Chart: Commanding and Requesting (Continued)

Type	*Sample sentences*	*Notes*
Direct Question	Can you cash this check? Could you cash this check? Will you please cash this? Would you please cash this for me?	Request. Polite.
	Do you mind cashing this? Would you mind cashing this?	Very polite. Most appropriate.
	Do you mind if I use your phone?	Asking for permission. Followed by present tense. Very polite.
	Would you mind if I used your phone?	Appropriate in all cases. Followed by past tense.
Indirect Question	I wonder if you would cash this check for me.	Request. Very polite.
	I wonder if you could cash this check for me.	Appropriate in all cases.
	I wonder if I could use your phone. I wonder if I might use your phone.	Asking for permission. Very polite. Appropriate in all cases. Follows sequence of tenses as in indirect speech.

Summary Chart: Refusing

Type	*Sample*
Statement + reason	No, it's not my turn to clean up and I won't do it.
I'm sorry, + excuse	I'm sorry I can't come, but I'm going away for the weekend.
Conditional + excuse	I woud lend you my notes, but I need them myself to study for the quiz.

UNIT III
ADVISING AND SUGGESTING, CAUTIONING

Giving Advice and Making Suggestions

Giving advice means telling people what you think they should do or should not do. Making a suggestion is very similar, but it is usually not as strong as giving advice.

Many forms can be used to give advice or make a suggestion. Let's take a look at a situation and the forms that can be used. John, a university student, is talking to a friend, Nadine, about a problem. He has to buy a birthday present for Marilyn and he needs some advice. Nadine suggests flowers.

Buy her some flowers.	I like flowers.	Flowers.	How about flowers?
(Imperative)	(Statement)	(Single word)	(Question)

These four forms are very common. Here are more ways for Nadine to make her suggestion.

If I were you, I'd buy flowers. ("If I were you" clause + Conditional)	You should get her flowers. (Strong Modals)	You could buy her flowers. (Weak Modals)

IMPERATIVE

Imperative sentences are generally associated in people's minds with "commands," but they are often used for advice and suggestions as well as for requests and invitations. Imperatives may be used by anyone giving advice; between people of the same age, an older person to a younger one, a younger person to an older one, strangers, or friends.

The degree of politeness is dependent on the intonation more than the form in giving advice. Since imperative sentences are generally short, they can sound brusque if the intonation is not polite.

Remember that the imperative is *never* used for requests or commands to a person in authority.

Listening In

A. Two friends are talking.

Tom: I want to give up smoking; I really do, but how do I stop?

Sam: Just quit—cold turkey.

Your Turn

1. What other suggestions can you think of to give Tom? Remember to use the imperative form.
2. Complete the following dialogues by giving your advice.
   a) Your friend says, "I've got to pass this course, I really do, but how do I do it? I don't understand anything about calculus."
   b) Your roommate says, "I can't decide which movie to see tonight."

B. A student is talking to his professor.

Jerry: Could you tell us the best way to review for the test tomorrow?

Professor: Study your class notes very carefully and review the exercises in the text.

Jerry: Thanks, Professor Marshall. See you tomorrow.

C. Two strangers meet in front of the school library.

Man on the street: Do you know how I can get to the Modern Art Museum from here?

Student: Go by subway—it's fastest.

Your Turn

What would you tell a stranger who asked you how to get to the train station?

D. Two friends are talking. They are students in Minneapolis.

Alice: My cousin is arriving from San Francisco this afternoon. Where should I take her tonight?

Pam: Take her to a night club.

OR

Invite some friends over to meet her.

OR

Go to a good restaurant.

Your Turn

Every student in the class may give a suggestion concerning where to take someone in the city where he/she is now living.

STATEMENT

Indirect statements are frequently used to give advice. They are polite and can be used in any situation. The advice is not being given directly and the hearer feels under no obligation to accept it. *Direct* statements using verbs such as "I advise," "I suggest," and "I recommend" are usually used in more formal or impersonal situations and in writing.

Let's look at a situation in which indirect advice might be given. If a friend asks you where he should take his parents for dinner, what would you say? His parents are visiting from out of town, and he'd like to take them to a nice restaurant. Your choice would be the Riverside Inn. You could say:

Notice how much more formal this usage is. The grammatical construction is not the same for these forms.

suggest / recommend + (that) + Pronoun + Simple form of the verb

advise + Pronoun + Infinitive

In a restaurant, a waiter will often say:

May I suggest the roast beef?
May I recommend the oysters?

I think the Riverside Inn is a good place.
The Riverside Inn is my favorite restaurant.
I like the food at the Riverside Inn.
The food is excellent at the Riverside Inn.
My brother always goes to the Riverside Inn.
I've heard the Riverside Inn is one of the best in town.
The Riverside Inn is supposed to be good.
I'd say the Riverside Inn would be a good choice.

On the other hand, if you were a visitor to town, and asked the tourist office for the name of a good local restaurant, they might say:

I suggest (that) you go to the Riverside Inn.
I recommend (that) you go to the Riverside Inn.
I advise you to go to the Riverside Inn.

Listening In

A. A woman is browsing in the school bookstore. She asks the salesperson for some advice on what to buy.

Woman: Excuse me. I'm looking for a present for my son. I have no idea what to get him. Can you help me?

Clerk: Is he a student here?

Woman: Yes.

Clerk: Does he like sports?

Woman: Well, he plays basketball and he jogs.

Clerk: I think a sweatshirt would be a good idea.

OR

T-shirts are popular.

OR

I'd say clothes are the best thing.

- What questions would you have asked the mother?

- What suggestions might you have made?
- Can you imagine such a conversation taking place in your own country? Why or why not? Discuss.

Your Turn

Using an indirect statement, give advice to the people in the following situations. Ask for more information before you offer your advice. Work in pairs.

1. Margaret wants to know what to buy her mother for her birthday.
2. Walter wants to know what to take to the Andersons' where he is having dinner tonight.

B. Marjorie is talking with her academic advisor.

Marjorie: I've already studied English for two semesters and I think I'm ready to begin my regular courses.

Advisor: I have the English Department's evaluation here. They have suggested that, although your spoken English is quite good, you take an advanced writing course.

Marjorie: I really don't think I need any more English.

Advisor: Well, I can only go by what the English Department recommends. I always urge students to take as much English as possible before beginning other courses.

Marjorie: Then you advise me to take the writing course?

Advisor: Yes. I strongly recommend that you follow your English instructor's advice.

This is an appropriate formal usage of *urge* and *recommend*. If the advisor and the student were on informal terms, his last speech might have been less formal:

I think you should follow your English instructor's advice.

- How many different ways does the advisor give advice?
- What direct statement verbs does the advisor use?
- Why does the advisor generally use direct rather than indirect statements?

SINGLE WORD OR PHRASE

A complete sentence is not always necessary when giving advice or making suggestions. It is quite common to use a single word or a short phrase. This is especially common when you are asked directly for your opinion or advice.

Listening In

Two classmates are talking.

Peter: Do you know of a good place to eat around the university?

Mike: How much do you want to spend?

Peter: Not much!

Mike: The Hamburger King, maybe.

OR

The Pizza Inn on Second Avenue.

Your Turn

Give advice to your friends, using single words or phrases.

1. Where's a good place to buy sweaters?
2. What's a good movie to see this weekend?
3. What's the best thing to order in this restaurant?
4. Which book should I read during semester break?

INTERROGATIVE

Another way of giving advice is to use the question form. Often this form seems more polite because it is indirect. Instead of telling the person what to do, you offer an idea or a choice.

Listening In

Harold does not know what he should buy Judy for her birthday. He asks his friend Tony for advice.

Harold: What should I buy Judy for her birthday?

Tony: Does she like to read?

Harold: I think so.

Tony: How about a best seller?

OR

Why don't you get her a mystery?

OR

What about a book of poetry?

Your Turn

A. Your friend can't decide on a major field of study. You give advice using the cues given.

1. What about
2. How about
3. Why not
4. Have you thought about

B. Give advice in the following situations, using the interrogative form.

1. A classmate wants to know how to prepare for tomorrow's quiz.
2. A friend wants to get in shape for the baseball tryouts.
3. A friend wants to know what to serve guests for dinner tomorrow night.
4. Your teacher wants to know what kind of car to buy.

What's Happening?

Study the following picture from a comic strip. Then answer the questions that follow.

ARCHIE

to tackle = to undertake
task = job
bulldozer = a tractor with a blade for clearing away land

1. What is the problem that Archie has to solve?
2. Is Jughead's advice practical? What would you advise Archie?

"IF I WERE YOU"

This form is less direct and therefore not so strong and somewhat more polite. This form can be used with friends, acquaintances, and strangers. Sometimes we omit the clause "If I were you" but it is understood.

Listening In

A. Two friends are talking.

Scott: I can't decide which play to go to tonight.

Elmer: I'd go see *The Mysterious Planet* (if I were you). It's really amusing.

The clause, "if I were you," can come first in the sentence or be placed at the end without any difference in meaning.

B. A tourist is asking for advice.

Tourist: Excuse me, please. What's the best way to get to the train station from here?

Native: (If I were you,) I'd take the subway. It's the quickest way. The stop is right across the street. The subway will take you within a block of the train station.

Your Turn

Give advice in the following situations, using conditionals, and "If I were you."

1. Your friend asks, "What should I do about this coffee stain on my suit?"
2. Your roommate asks, "Where should I take my friend to dinner tonight?"
3. Your friend asks, "I want to go somewhere really exciting for my vacation this year. Any ideas?"

STRONG MODALS

"Should," "had better," and "ought to" are used to give strong advice. "Really" makes the advice stronger and more forceful. The addition of "perhaps" or "maybe" softens the advice and makes it more polite.

"Really" is placed before the strong modal in order to increase the force of the modal.

Listening In

Two students are discussing their math class.

Tai: I think I'll cut math class tomorrow.

Ricardo: You really should go to class. Mr. Johnson will notice if you're absent again.

Tai: But his class is so boring!

Ricardo: Maybe you ought to study harder, Tai. Then you might find the class more interesting.

Your Turn

Your friend, Molly, has a habit of never doing her homework. You're worried that she will flunk out of school. Complete the following sentences and advise her.

1. You'd better
2. You ought to
3. Maybe you should

WEAK MODALS

"Might" and "could" can be used if your opinion is not very strong or if you don't want to seem too pushy. Sentences with these modals are more indirect and therefore more polite.

Listening In

A. Two friends are talking.

Dick: Where can I take Kate tonight after the show?

Kim: You might take her to Tony's. They've got great pizza.

Dick: We went there last Saturday night.

Kim: You could go to the Tower for a sundae.

B. A student is talking to the teacher.

Student: I can't decide on a topic for my oral report. I'd like to do some research on the status of women in society.

Teacher: Well, you could discuss the role of women in your culture. Or you might give your impression of American women and their influence on society.

If the teacher said: "You should discuss the role of women" that would be strong and probably be understood as an order rather than as advice.

If the teacher used a question: "Would you like to discuss the role of women?" the student might feel it necessary to decide at once.

Your Turn

Give advice in the situations below, using a weak modal.

1. Your friend can't decide what to order for lunch.
2. Your classmate doesn't know how to explain to the teacher why yesterday's assignment is late.

What's Happening?

Divide into small groups of three or four and discuss the comic strip. Answer the questions that follow.

Dad = father
keep in mind = remember, consider

WEE PALS by MORRIE TURNER

1. Why is Randy surprised to hear his mother say "your dad 'suggests'"?
2. Did Randy interpret his father's "suggestion" as a suggestion?

SUMMING UP: ADVISING AND SUGGESTING

Listening In

Bill: What should I give Antonia for a graduation present?

Jeff: Perfume.

Bill: I don't know what kind she likes.

Jeff: Buy her a sweater then.

Bill: I don't know her size.

Jeff: Let me think. How about a book?

Bill: No.

Jeff: I give up. I think you'd better ask *her* what she'd like.

Bill: Then it wouldn't be a surprise. Come on, help me! I'm getting desperate.

Jeff: You could ask her roommate. She probably knows what Toni likes.

Bill: Her roommate's no help; I've already asked her.

Jeff: Good grief! Hey, wait a minute! Get her a gift certificate.

Bill: Hey! Not a bad idea. I could get a gift certificate at her favorite store. That would solve the problem. Thanks, Jeff. You are a genius!

- What is the relationship between Bill and Jeff?
- What suggestions and advice does Jeff give? What forms does he use?
- Do you think a gift certificate is an appropriate gift? Would it be an acceptable gift in your culture? Discuss.

Your Turn

A. Complete the sentences for this situation. Your friend has lost his house key. Advise him.

1. Try
2. I think
3. Why not
4. Call
5. I would
6. How about

B. Give the same advice twice in the situations below, but use two different forms.

1. Your friend asks what she should serve at a dinner party.
2. Your teacher wants to have a party for the class. Suggest a good time to have it.
3. Your roommate wants to know what to wear to a party tonight.

Appropriate Responses

Choose one of the following responses, and explain why you feel that your choice is the most appropriate and why the other responses are not appropriate.

1. Your friend asks for some ideas as to what to serve at the party he's giving.
   - a) I advise you to serve wine.
   - b) I would recommend that you serve wine.
   - c) Why don't you serve wine?
2. Your roommate asks you where he could take his girlfriend this weekend.
   - a) I would recommend that you go to a movie.
   - b) Why not go roller skating?
   - c) May I suggest that you take her to a nice restaurant?

Role Plays

A. Choose a partner. Prepare dialogues for the following situations.

1. Ask your classmate how to get an "A" in math.
2. Ask your teacher to suggest an interesting place for you to visit this weekend. You don't know the city very well.
3. Ask your neighbor to tell you where to go grocery shopping in your area.
4. You're afraid you won't be able to finish your research paper on time. Ask your friend to give you some advice on how to study more efficiently.

B. Choose a partner and then prepare dialogues of 6–8 exchanges that you and your partner will perform orally in front of the class.

1. Imagine two friends are talking. Friend A wants to drop out of school for a semester to earn some money. Friend B tries to persuade A not to by offering some sound advice.
2. Imagine a situation in which one person is seeking advice and the other one is offering it.

Your Turn

Another way to do this is to have students write their problems on pieces of paper and hand them in to the instructor. The instructor can then read the problems and let the class carry on the discussion from that point.

Think of a real problem that you have. Ask your classmates for advice. They will try to give you helpful advice.

Examples:

I want to learn to speak English well, but at home I speak only my native language.

I need to buy a textbook for my course, but the bookstore ran out of it.

I get so nervous before a test or exam that I can't do my best work. I seem to forget everything that I've studied.

What's Happening?

Divide up into small groups of three or four. Discuss the following comic strip.

carbohydrates = starches and sugars

1. Sometimes we are not sure at first if a statement is an order or a piece of advice. Is Dagwood ordering or advising Alexander not to eat any more doughnuts?
2. With a partner, rewrite this comic strip twice. First change the dialogue so that it is clear from the beginning that Dagwood is issuing an order. Then change it so that Dagwood is giving advice. You may change the ending in either or both versions.

Role Plays

A. Characters: Steve
Judy

Steve has just received his income tax refund check in the mail. It is a check for $500.00. He *suggests* that he and his girlfriend Judy celebrate. Judy, a cautious person, *advises* Steve not to get too excited. She *suggests* several ways in which he could use the money. Steve ignores her advice and has several other *suggestions* of his own. Judy becomes a little impatient with Steve and strongly *advises* him not to waste the money on something foolish. Steve finally decides to (make up your own ending).

B. Characters: Luis
Phil

Luis and his roommate Phil are looking forward to their two-month summer vacation. Luis asks Phil for some *suggestions* on how to spend this time. Luis doesn't like any of Phil's suggestions so he thinks of a few *suggestions* of his own. Luis *suggests* that they cross the United States by bus. Phil *advises* Luis not to consider traveling by bus because it would take too long. Luis then *suggests* renting a car for the trip, but Phil *recommends* that they travel by plane. Luis reminds his roommate that they have only two months of vacation; he *advises* him to make up his mind before the summer is over.

Cautioning

A caution is given to let someone know of an imminent or possible danger or risk. An attempt is made to warn the person in time so that he/she can avoid a dangerous or unpleasant situation. You can see that a caution is a special kind of advice and uses some of the same forms, but it is advice that is intended to keep something dangerous or unpleasant from happening.

The choice of form to use will depend on whether there is immediate danger or not, how forceful you want to be, and who you are speaking to. Let's take a look at a situation and the forms that can be used. Mike is driving his friend, Jose, home from school. It has just begun to snow rather heavily. Jose can say:

Slow down! It's starting to snow.
(Imperative)

You'd better drive more slowly in the snow.
(Strong Modal)

It's necessary to drive very slowly when it's snowing.
(Statement)

If I were you, I'd slow down. It's snowing.
("If I were you" clause + Conditional)

IMPERATIVE

This form is very direct and strong; it must be used when the situation calls for an urgent warning, whether you are speaking to a friend, a superior, or a stranger.

Listening In

A. Two friends are about to cross a busy street.

Todd: Watch out! Don't cross the street now! There's a car coming.
Mike: Thanks! I was so busy talking that I didn't even realize the light was red.

B. Two strangers are about to cross a busy street.

Todd: Look out for the car!
Stranger: Thank you for warning me. I didn't see it.

STRONG MODALS

Strong modals (ought to, should, must, have to, had better) are commonly used for cautions. Weak modals are never used.

Listening In

A. Two friends are talking:

Nancy: You shouldn't smoke so much. Cigarettes are bad for your health.
Aaron: I know but I just can't seem to kick the habit.

B. Mr. Johnston is at the gas station.

Attendant: You'd better put out that cigarette, sir.
Mr. Johnston: Oh, I'm sorry. Sure.

Your Turn

Give warnings in the following situations using an imperative or a modal.

1. Your friend is about to take a sip of very hot coffee. You don't want her to burn her tongue.
2. Your roommate is about to drink his fifth glass of beer. He's supposed to drive you home after the party.
3. Warn your roommate that Mr. Donaldson gives difficult reading tests.
4. Tell your friends to stop playing soccer because you have just seen lightning.
5. Tell your friend not to eat at the Club Cafe. Give a reason.

STATEMENTS

An indirect statement implies a caution.

"It's not safe to use those stairs."

A direct statement clearly states a caution.

"I'm warning you (that) those stairs are not safe."
"I'm telling you (that) those stairs are not safe."

A direct statement used as a caution is very strong; it may also be used in a hostile way.

One man to another in an argument:

"I'm warning you, you'd better not come any closer."

This implies that something bad will happen if he *does* come closer.

Listening In

Two friends are talking at a party.

Suzanne: Jenny, I'm leaving now.

Jenny: Do you have a ride?

Suzanne: No. That's OK. It's not far. I'll walk.

Jenny: It's not safe to walk alone at this time of night.

Suzanne: I'm not nervous.

Jenny: But it's really dangerous. Let me give you a ride.

"IF I WERE YOU" + CONDITIONAL

These clauses are used for warnings that are less direct and that are usually, but not always, more polite.

Listening In

A. A father and son are talking.

Jack: If I were you, Dad, I wouldn't eat any more of that fish. I think maybe it's spoiled.

Dad: I think you're right. It has a peculiar taste.

B. Two friends are chatting during a movie.

Stranger: If I were you, I would stop talking before the usher asks you to leave.

Friends: Oh, we're sorry.

Sometimes "If I were you" is omitted but it is understood.

C. Two friends are talking.

Laura: I wouldn't drive to the picnic with Leslie. She's such a reckless driver.

Kit: She is? I didn't know that. Thanks for warning me.

Your Turn

A. Complete the following sentences.

1. Your friend is driving too fast.
   a) If I were you,
   b) I'm warning you,
2. Your classmate doesn't want to study for the grammar test.
   a) If I were you,
   b) I'm telling you,

B. Substitute "If I were you" plus a conditional for each caution in the sentences below.

Example: Don't take that course. It's awful.
If I were you, I wouldn't take that course; it's awful.

1. You shouldn't eat so much. People who are overweight are more likely to have heart attacks.
2. I'm warning you, you'd better not call Claire after 10 p.m. It annoys her.

SUMMING UP: CAUTIONING

Listening In

Lee: Have you studied for tomorrow's math test yet?

Joe: I sure have. I spent all weekend studying.

Lee: Well, I haven't opened a book yet.

Joe: Are you kidding? You'd better start studying. You know you can't pass Professor Olsen's tests without studying.

Lee: But I want to go to the hockey game tonight.

Joe: I'm telling you, the test will be tough.

Lee: I guess it's too late to start studying anyway.

Joe: If I were you, I'd really work hard tonight.

Lee: I sure hate to miss that game but . . . .

Joe: Listen! Go to the game and I know you'll be sorry.

Lee: I guess you're right. Let's grab a bite to eat and then I'll go to the library.

Joe: OK. Let's go!

- Who are the speakers? What is their relationship?
- Reread the dialogue aloud, substituting a different form for each caution.

Your Turn

Prepare a short dialogue for each situation.

1. Caution your friend that the police on campus give lots of parking tickets.
2. You are a teacher at a university. Warn the students not to cheat on the exam.
3. Warn a stranger on the street that the sidewalk is slippery.
4. Your friend wants to take a course that you had last semester. Caution her that it is a lot of work.

Role Play (advice, suggestions and cautions)

Characters: Five friends who are students in the same class at school. The actors in the role play may substitute their own names for the letters below.

The students are having a midterm exam in English next week. Student A *suggests* that the five of them study together. Student B says he doesn't plan to study for the midterm. Student C *advises* him that it is important to pass the exam. Student D *cautions* Student B that his parents will be furious if he fails the exam. Student E *warns* Student B that his grade average in the course is very low. Student C *suggests* that Student A prepare some coffee. Student B *cautions* Student A not to make it too strong. Student B *cautions* him not to make it too weak. Student A *suggests* that he does not need so much advice on how to make the coffee. As they drink the coffee, each student offers advice on how best to study for the exam. Student D *suggests* that they meet at 3 p.m. tomorrow afternoon to start studying. Student E *advises* everyone to bring his own textbook, paper, and a pencil. Everyone agrees. The meeting breaks up and everyone goes home for dinner.

Summary Chart: Advising

Type	*Sample sentences*	*Notes*
Imperative	Wear your red dress to the party.	Usually in response to a direct request for advice.
Statement —indirect	I like roses. McDonald's is cheap. Ice skating is always fun.	Usually in response to a direct request for advice.
—direct	I suggest (that) you study for the test. I urge you to study for the test. I recommend (that) you study for the test. I advise you to study for the test.	Formal The simple form of the verb is used after "suggest" and "recommend" while the infinitive is used after "urge" and "advise."
Question	Why (don't you) stay home tonight? (not) Don't you think you should stay home? Don't you think it would be better to stay home? Don't you think it would be better if you stayed home? Wouldn't it be better to stay home? Wouldn't it be better if you stayed home? Wouldn't it be a good idea if you stayed home? What about staying home? (How)	Weak/More polite/Informal. "Better" can be followed by an infinitive phrase or by an if-clause. "What about" and "how about" are followed by the -ing form of the verb.
	Have you thought about staying home?	Weak/Informal.
	Have you considered staying home? May I suggest (that) you stay home? (recommend that) May I advise you to stay home? (urge)	Formal/Weak/Often used in writing "Suggest" and "recommend" are followed by the simple form of the verb while "advise" and "urge" are followed by the infinitive.

Summary Chart: Advising (Continued)

Type	*Sample sentences*	*Notes*
"If I were you" + Conditional	If I were you, I'd go to the new Italian restaurant. I'd go to the new Italian restaurant.	The order of the clauses may be reversed; "I'd go to the new Italian restaurant, (if I were you)."
Strong Modals	You ought to get some sleep. should had better	Strong. The simple form of the verb follows the modal.
Weak Modals	You might try the spaghetti. could	Weak. The simple form of the verb follows the modal.

Summary Chart: Cautioning

Type	*Sample sentences*	*Notes*
Imperative	Be careful! The coffee's hot. Watch out! There's a car coming. Leave me alone or I'll call the police.	
Strong Modals	You must get more exercise. You'd better clean up that mess.	
Statement	I'm warning you, (stop bothering me.) I'm telling you, (you'd better leave.)	Statements like "I'm warning you" are generally followed by an imperative sentence or one with a strong modal.
"If I were you" + Conditional	If I were you, I'd stop smoking.	The clause may be reversed: "I'd stop smoking if I were you.

PROMISING, APOLOGIZING, EXPRESSING REGRET AND SYMPATHIZING

Promising

A promise is a declaration to another person that you will or will not do something, or that something definitely will or will not happen.

Look at these possible ways to make a promise. Jan promises to return Penny's book.

I'll bring it tomorrow.	If you call me tonight, I'll bring it tomorrow.	Count on me. I won't forget it.
(Statement)	("If" clause)	(Imperative)

STATEMENTS

The most common and simplest way to promise is to use the future tense "will." Contractions (*I'll* and *we'll*) are frequently used. Also special verbs and expressions are used to make promises; they make a promise clearer or more forceful.

Listening In

A. Nancy has taken her typewriter to the repair shop to be fixed.

Repairman: It doesn't look like a serious problem. We'll have it ready for you by next Tuesday.

Nancy: That's awful! I have a paper due on Monday and I really need to have it this weekend.

Repairman: Well, if it's an emergency, I'll try to work on it right away. Come back on Friday. I'll have it fixed by then.

Nancy: Are you sure?

Repairman: I promise you it will be ready on Friday.

- How many promises are there in the dialogue? Identify them.

Word order. It is also possible to reverse the order of the clauses. In the dialogue the repairman says, "I promise you it will be ready on Friday." He could have said: "It will be ready on Friday, I promise."

Special Verbs and Expressions. Here are four ways to make a promise more direct:

I promise (you) (that) it'll be ready on Friday.
I assure you (that) it will be ready on Friday.
I give you my word (that) it'll be ready on Friday.
You have my word (that) it will be ready on Friday.

If "that" is omitted, the meaning of the sentence is not changed.

Useful expressions:

To make a promise = to promise something to someone

He made a promise to his parents that he would finish school before getting married.

To keep a promise = to do what you promised to do

He kept his promise to his parents

To break a promise = not to do what you promised to do

"My boss promised to give me a raise, but broke her promise."

Your Turn

1. Pretend that you are going to borrow your friend's car. He needs to use it at 8:00. Promise him that you will return it by 7:30.

   Use the four ways given above to make your promise more forceful.

2. Promise a classmate that you'll meet later to study for the exam.

   a) I'll meet you later. ______________________.
   b) ______________ to meet you later.
   c) ______________ (that) I'll meet you later.

B. Two classmates are talking.

Natalie: You promised to help me with my grammar homework this week, but you haven't kept your promise.

Jean: I'm sorry, I can't do it today, but I swear I'll help you tomorrow, OK?

Natalie: I guess so, but I'm really getting worried about the exam, so please don't forget.

Jean: I swear I won't.

- Why does Jean make such a strong promise, in your opinion?

The expression "I swear" is a very strong way of promising.

C. A customer is looking at new cars.

Salesperson: I guarantee that this car will get 35 miles to the gallon on the highway.

Customer: Really? That's good!

The verb "guarantee" is often used when discussing merchandise or services in business contexts.

Examples:

a. The company guarantees that this refrigerator will last for 10 years.
b. The furniture repair company guarantees its repairs for six months.

Students can bring guarantees or warranties in to class for discussion.

"IF" CLAUSES

We sometimes make promises with conditions attached. We use "if" clauses to make promises which will be kept only if the condition is met. The promise is in the future tense but the condition is in either present or future tense.

Listening In

A. Two friends are talking.

Barbara: Can you give me a ride to the game tomorrow?

Todd: I'll give you a ride if you'll help pay for the gas.

Barbara: Sure.

B. A teacher and a student are talking.

Student: I have to pass this course or I'll be put on academic probation.

Teacher: I can't promise you'll pass but if your exam grade is high, you'll get a "C" in the course.

Student: I guess I'd better study hard then.

C. Two roommates are talking.

Sally: I'll cook dinner tonight if you'll do the laundry.

Ann: That's fine with me.

Your Turn

Complete the following "if" clauses by supplying the promises or the condition attached.

1. Teacher to students:
   I'll let you go home early today if you ____________ .
2. You to your neighbor's child:
   If you ____________ I'll give you some ice cream.
3. A student to his friend:
   ____________ if you lend me your notes.
4. A girl to her roommate:
   If you let me wear your new jeans, ____________ .

IMPERATIVES

There are several imperative expressions which we can use to emphasize the fact that we are promising something. They make the promises stronger. Look at these examples.

I'll have the paper typed by Sunday. Count on it.
I'll be on time. Believe me.
I'll bring your book tomorrow. Trust me.

Listening In

A. Two classmates are talking

Albert: We're having a meeting at 4:00 to plan the end-of-semester party. We really need more people to help.

Juan: I'll be there. Count on me.

"To count on" means "to depend on." In other words, Juan is promising Albert that he will be at the meeting. He could also say, "Count on me to be there." or "I'll be there. Count on it."

B. Two sisters are talking.

Jean: I won't tell your secret to anyone. Believe me!

Ruth: And trust me not to say a word about your secret either.

Your Turn

Use the verbs in the parentheses to complete the following promises.

1. We'll go shopping after class. _____________ (count)
2. I won't get into an accident. _____________ (trust)
3. _____________ to go to the movies with you tomorrow. (count)
4. _____________ . I'll tell you the truth. (believe)

SUMMING UP: PROMISING

Your Turn

A. Complete these dialogues using promises. Choose a partner.

1. You are in a store looking at calculators.

Salesperson: May I help you?

You: Yes. I can't decide whether to buy this calculator or not. I like it, but it seems kind of expensive.

Salesperson: It's a good investment. _____________ .

2. You are talking to your teacher.

   Teacher: What are you worried about?

   You: Well, I'm worried about my scholarship. Do you think I'll get an "A" this semester?

   Teacher: It's hard to say right now, but if ____________ .

3. You are talking to your roommate.

   You: I'd rather do 500 math problems than clean this messy apartment.

   Roommate: Not me. I hate math, but I don't mind cleaning.

   You: I have an idea! I'll ____________ .

B. For each of the following situations use two different forms of promises. Do NOT use the word "promise." Practice using a variety of forms.

1. Promise your teacher you won't be late for class anymore.
2. Your friend has a very serious personal problem but is afraid to tell anyone. Promise that you won't tell anyone about it.
3. A friend is planning to move into another apartment next weekend. Promise to help.

What's Happening?

Divide up into small groups of three or four. Discuss the comic strip below.

Sarge = abbreviated form of sergeant, a military rank

Hold it! = Wait! Stop!

1. Locate the promise in this comic strip.
2. Is this promise kept?
3. Are Sarge's favorite foods popular in your country?
4. Can you explain the common expression "As American as apple pie"?
5. What function does the expression "Hold it!" have in this dialogue? How else could you say the same thing using a different expression?

Apologizing

An apology is a statement of regret for doing something wrong, for being impolite, or for hurting someone's feelings. An apology indicates that you're sorry for something which you did, or for something which you did not do. For example, you have just bumped into your friend in the cafeteria, and her cup of coffee has spilled on the floor.

I'm really sorry. I wasn't watching where I was going. I'll keep my eyes open. Let me get you a new cup.
(Parts of an apology)

"Excuse me" is often used simply to get someone's attention, rather than as an apology.
(Use of "excuse me")

If you had said: "I'm sorry, but you were right in my way," that would *not* be an apology.
(I'm sorry, but)

Your friend could answer: That's OK.
(Accepting and refusing apologies)

PARTS OF AN APOLOGY

An apology may be simply "I'm sorry" or it might be more complex. Let's look at the four parts an apology might have. (It is not necessary to use all four parts in every apology. An apology might have one, two, three, or four parts.)

1. An expression of regret or a request for forgiveness

   Examples: I'm really sorry.
   Please forgive me.
   I apologize.

2. An excuse, a reason, or a statement of responsibility

   Examples: It was my own fault. I was so tired last night that I forgot to set my alarm clock.
   I didn't mean to do it.
   I was so busy that I forgot.

3. A promise to improve or a promise not to do it again

   Examples: I assure you it will never happen again.
   I give you my word I'll be on time from now on.
   I promise I won't forget again.

4. An offer to do something to improve the situation

   Examples: I'll stay late tonight to finish the report.
   I'll buy you a new dish.

Listening In

A. An employee apologizes to his/her employer.

Employer: It's 10:00! You know the budget report has to be ready by tomorrow morning. You promised to be here early today.

Employee: I'm really sorry. It's my own fault. I was so tired last night that I forgot to set my alarm clock. I assure you it will never happen again. I'll stay late tonight to finish the report.

Employer: All right. Now let's get right to work.

Your Turn

Two students will change the dialogue above so that the characters are a student and professor. The dialogue will change somewhat but the apology should still have four parts to it. The situation should remain the same; the student is late to class.

B. Two friends are talking. Sharon has just returned Arthur's car. The gas tank is almost empty.

Arthur: I don't mind your borrowing my car, but gas is really expensive now, you know.

Sharon: I was in a hurry. I'll fill the tank right now.

- What does Arthur really mean by saying, "Gas is really expensive now"?
- Can you find the apology in the dialogue?
- How does Sharon show that she is sorry? What parts of an apology does she use?

C. Adrian and Mark are playing baseball in front of their apartment building. Suddenly their baseball goes smashing through a neighbor's window. Adrian reluctantly goes and knocks on the lady's door.

Mrs. Minton: Yes?

Adrian: I'm very sorry. My ball just went through your window.

Mrs. Minton: (angrily) So, it was *your* ball.

Adrian: We didn't mean to do it. It was an accident. We'll pay for the damages.

- Why is Adrian apologizing?
- How does he show that his apology is sincere?
- Does he give an excuse for what he did?
- What does he offer to do?
- Why do you think Mark lets Adrian do all the explaining?

We can use adverbs (intensifiers) to make our apologies stronger or more sincere.

Examples: I'm very sorry.
I'm really sorry.
I'm terribly sorry.
I'm awfully sorry.
I'm extremely sorry.

Your Turn

Practice the following ways of apologizing. Show that you did not intend to do something by apologizing to your classmate for something. Work in pairs.

I didn't mean to do it.
It was an accident.
It wasn't intentional.
I didn't do it on purpose.

"I didn't mean to" means that you did not intend to do it. This phrase is often added to an apology. Note the similar phrases that are given in the exercise.

D. Archie forgot a dinner date with Betty. They run into each other the next day.

Betty: What happened to you last night?

Archie: What do you mean?

Betty: Don't you remember? You promised to take me to dinner last night.

Archie: Oh, I'm sorry. I completely forgot. Rex came over and we went to the stadium.

Betty: Forgot?! How could you?

Archie: I didn't do it on purpose.

Archie: I swear I'll never be so stupid again. How about going to dinner tonight instead?

Betty: OK. I guess I'll forgive you this time, but only if you never do it again.

- Why is Betty angry?
- How does Archie apologize? Find two apologies.
- What excuse does he give?
- What promise does he make?
- What offer does he make in order to pacify Betty?

"Forgive me" is another way to apologize. Usually it is used for more serious discourtesies such as hurting someone's feelings or doing something wrong.

It is usually used in close, personal relationships such as between husband and wife, girl friend and boyfriend, intimate friends, etc.

If we use a verb after "forgive," we must use "for" + ing verb. Look at the following examples:

Please forgive me *for forgetting* our date.

Forgive me *for breaking* my promise.

Your Turn

Use "forgive" in the following situations.

1. You forgot your close friend's birthday. Apologize and then make a promise.
2. You promised to visit your friend on Sunday. A special meal had been cooked for you. You forgot about the invitation. Apologize. Then make a promise. Then offer to do something to make it up to your friend.

E. Mr. Davis arrives late for a job interview.

Mr. Davis: I must apologize for being late. I had trouble finding this address. Please accept my apologies.

Mrs. Wang: The position has already been filled. You are two hours late.

- Does Mr. Davis have a valid excuse?
- Does Mrs. Wang accept his apologies?
- Is punctuality very important in your culture?

SUMMING UP: PARTS OF AN APOLOGY

Listening In

Yesterday Marie and John had an argument. Now John sees Marie walking toward the library.

John: Marie! Wait! I want to talk to you.

Marie: I told you I never wanted to see you again.

John: Listen! I'm sorry for all those things I said last night. Let's bury the hatchet.

Marie: No way.

John: I really mean it. I'm sorry. Can't you forgive me? What do you say? Let's kiss and make up.

Marie: Oh, all right. I guess I can forgive and forget if you can.

Idiomatic Expressions

Here are some idioms which you can use if you have been quarreling or arguing with someone and you want to apologize and be friends again.

Examples:

Let's let bygones be bygones. (that is, let's forget our past disagreements)

Let's kiss and make up. (only for "romantic" friends)

Let's forgive and forget.

Let's bury the hatchet.

John: Great! Let's go get an ice cream cone to celebrate.

- What idioms are used in this dialogue to apologize?
- What other forms of apology can you find?

USE OF "EXCUSE ME"

"Excuse me" or "Pardon me" are not used in exactly the same way as "I'm sorry" or "I apologize."

"Excuse me" or "Pardon me" are used only when we interrupt someone, or break a minor social rule such as sneezing or burping, pushing in front of someone who is in our way, or try to get someone's attention.

"I'm sorry" and "I apologize" are used for more serious mistakes or discourtesies such as hurting someone or causing someone serious difficulty.

Listening In

A. Jill has just finished eating in a restaurant. She is in a hurry to leave, but the waitress hasn't brought the check yet. She sees the waitress a few feet away.

Jill: Excuse me. Could I please have the check?

Waitress: Of course.

- Why does Jill say "Excuse me"?
- How does the waitress respond?

How do you get someone's attention in your country? By snapping your fingers? By clapping? By whistling?

In the United States, none of these ways is polite. The best way to get the attention of a waiter, waitress or salesperson is by saying "Excuse me" or "Pardon me." Non-verbally, you might establish eye contact or you could raise your hand slightly.

B. Karen and Susan are talking in Susan's home.

Karen: Have you see Joe lately?

Susan: No, I haven't. He . . . (telephone rings) Oh, excuse me a second.

Karen: Sure.

- Why does Susan say "Excuse me"?
- Would you have apologized in your culture?

C. Two strangers are waiting for a bus.

Woman: Excuse me. Do you have the time, please?

Man: Yes. It's 2:37.

Woman: Thank you.

- Why does the woman say "Excuse me"?

D. A group of students are standing in front of a classroom building, blocking the entrance. Harry has to get inside to go to class.

Harry: (to the students) Excuse me.

Student: Sure.

- What does Harry want the students to do?

SUMMING UP: EXCUSE ME

Your Turn

Excuse yourself in each of these situations.

1. You are a stranger in town. Ask a passer-by how to get to the Ritz Hotel.
2. You are at the theater. In order to get to your seat in the middle of the row, you have to pass several people already sitting down.
3. You are in a crowded department store. Try to get the clerk's attention.

APOLOGIES WITH "I'M SORRY BUT" CLAUSES

Sometimes our apologies are given only to be polite or civil to another person, even though we are not really sorry about the situation, or when we are justifying our behavior. We use an "I'm sorry but" clause to soften an order, a decision, a criticism, or a refusal.

Listing In

A. Various situations

Test monitor to Students	I'm sorry, but your time is up. Put your pencils down. (order)
Security Guard to Passenger	I'm sorry, sir, but you'll have to open that suitcase. (order)
Interviewer to Applicant	I'm sorry, but your application cannot be considered. (refusal)
Teacher to Student	I'm sorry, but your handwriting is just too difficult to read. (criticism)
Employer to Job Applicant	I'm sorry, but we've hired someone else. (decision)
Teacher to Class	I'm sorry, but I have no other choice. We have to cancel this course. There are only 3 students enrolled. (decision)

B. Two roommates meet in class.

Roy: I couldn't get into the apartment this afternoon.

Steve: I'm sorry, but I warned you not to forget your keys again.

Roy: Why didn't you just leave it open?

Steve: Well, I'm very sorry, but I didn't want to do that. It's too risky.

- What excuses/reasons does Steve give for locking his roommate out?
- Does he really feel sorry about it?

C. Two roommates are talking.

Richard: Why didn't you wake me up this morning? I missed my exam and got an "F."

Tim: Well, I'm sorry, but you deserved it. I told you a hundred times last night to set your alarm. I had to leave earlier than usual, so I couldn't wake you up.

- Is Richard justified in being angry with Tim?
- If you were Tim, would you be sorry for Richard?

D. Two friends are talking after class.

Ron: What a surprise! Why didn't you tell me there was a test today? Thanks a lot!

Norman: Wait a minute! I'm sorry, but it isn't my fault you're never home when I try to call you.

- Is Ron sincere when he thanks Norman?

What's Happening?

Divide up into groups of three or four. Discuss the comic strip below.

1. Why does the elevator man apologize?
2. Does the boss accept his apology?
3. Why is this comic strip humorous?
4. Is Dagwood polite when he gives orders to his boss and to the elevator man? Explain.

SUMMING UP: I'M SORRY BUT

Your Turn

Apologize in each situation and use the "I'm sorry but" clause.

1. Pretend that you are a teacher. Explain to a student that he/she failed to pass the final exam and has to repeat the course.
2. Pretend that you are a tenant. You have to tell your landlady that your check from home is late and you can't pay the rent.
3. Pretend that you are a salesclerk. Tell the customer that it is impossible to fix his camera by the next morning.

ACCEPTING AND REFUSING APOLOGIES

After someone has apologized, the other person responds by accepting or refusing the apology.

Expressions for Accepting Apologies

That's OK.
I understand.
Don't worry about it.
It doesn't matter.
It's not important.
Don't mention it.
No problem. (informal)

Listening In

A. Two friends are talking.

Jane: I'm sorry I forgot to call you.

Carol: That's OK. We can meet after class and talk.

B. A student and teacher are talking.

Student: I would like to apologize for not paying attention in class today. I didn't sleep very well last night.

Teacher: I understand. We all have bad days. I hope you feel better tomorrow.

Apologies are usually accepted. A refusal is a very negative statement.

C. Another student and the same teacher are talking.

Student: I'm sorry I was talking during class. I won't do it again.

Teacher: You know, this isn't the first time I've had to ask you to be quiet. I'm really getting tired of your rude behavior.

- Why do you think the teacher reacts differently to the two students?
- Were both students polite?

SUMMING UP: ACCEPTING AND REFUSING APOLOGIES

Role Play

Choose a partner. Prepare dialogues for the following situations.

1. Apologize to your neighbor for the loud party in your apartment the night before.
2. Apologize to your employer for not having the reports copied. Explain that the copying machine is broken.
3. You are a mechanic. Apologize to your customer for not having her car ready. Tell her that the replacement part will be in the next day.
4. Apologize to the people who live across the street. Your dog has just dug up their prize roses.

Expressing Regret and Sympathizing

When you regret something, it means that you are sorry about something which you did or didn't do. It is different from an apology because you are not apologizing to someone else, but simply stating something you wish had been different. Let's take a look at a situation in which two friends are discussing their last semester in school.

I'm sorry I didn't study harder for my tests.

OR

I wish I had studied harder for my tests.

I'm sorry I didn't take French this semester.

OR

I wish I had taken French this semester.

We say "I'm sorry" when we have done something wrong or impolite. We also say "I'm sorry" when someone else has been hurt by an event or a situation and we want to sympathize with them. Look at these possible ways to express regret or sympathy.

I'm so sorry to hear that your grandmother died.
I'm very sorry that you didn't get accepted to law school.
I'm sorry Alex was so rude to you today.

Listening In

Two friends are talking on the telephone.

Carol: Lucy? Hi. I tried to call earlier.

Lucy: Oh, hi, Carol. Yeah. Well, I lost my purse today . . . and

Carol: No! Was there a lot of money in it?

Lucy: I had just cashed a check from my dad.

Carol: What a shame.

Lucy: Yeah, and it was for my tuition.

Carol: How awful!

- How many times does Carol express sympathy?
- Can you think of any other expressions that Carol could have used?

Sympathizing with "Conversation Fillers"

There are numerous short expressions we use throughout a conversation with someone where sympathizing is appropriate. By using these expressions we give reinforcement and encouragement to the unhappy person.

Examples:

No!	That's too bad.
How awful!	What a shame.
I can't believe it.	I'm sorry.

Your Turn

Choose partners. Students will tell their partners about something unhappy or upsetting that happened to them recently. The other student will practice sympathizing using appropriate conversation fillers.

SUMMING UP: APOLOGIZING, EXPRESSING REGRET AND SYMPATHIZING

Your Turn

A. Complete the following apologies.

1. ____________ that I broke your flower pot.
2. ____________ for not sending you a postcard from Africa.
3. I'm sorry ____________ .
4. Sorry. I didn't mean ____________ .
5. Excuse me ____________ .
6. I apologize ____________ .
7. Will you forgive me ____________ ?
8. I would like to ____________ .
9. Let me ____________ .
10. Forgive me ____________ .

B. Give appropriate apologies for each situation.

1. You forgot about a friend's dinner invitation. Your friend is upset. Apologize. Give a reason or explanation. Promise to do something to make it up to him/her.
2. You borrowed your classmate's textbook and you lost it. Apologize. Make a promise or an offer.
3. You have to tell your professor that your assignment will be late. Apologize. Explain.

4. You must leave your friend's party early. Express your regret and give a reason. Then say good-bye.
5. You have just spilled hot coffee on a stranger in the cafeteria. Apologize. Offer to do something.
6. You borrowed a friend's car and had a minor accident. There's a dent in the fender. Apologize. Offer to do something.

Appropriate Responses

Choose an appropriate apology for each situation.

1. You stepped on a stranger's foot on the subway.
   a) Excuse me.
   b) Oh, I'm really sorry. Are you all right?
   c) I'm sorry.
   d) It won't happen again.
2. You borrowed your professor's lab manual and you lost it.
   a) I'm very sorry. I'll be glad to pay for it.
   b) Excuse me, please.
   c) Please accept my apologies.
   d) Can you forgive me?

Role Plays

A. Prepare dialogues of 6–8 exchanges with another student. Then perform it for the rest of the class.
   1. A must apologize to B for arriving two hours late for dinner. A and B are good friends so they have an informal relationship. (Substitute your names for A and B.)
   2. A goes into a gift shop and breaks an expensive china cup. B is the owner of the shop.

B. Before you begin to prepare this role play, locate all the instances where an apology would be in order.

Characters: Sarah
Harry
Jack
Debbie

Sarah is having a party to celebrate her birthday. Harry arrives on time, but he has forgotten to buy a present for Sarah. Jack arrives on time, but he has left her present in the car and has to go back to get it. Debbie arrives late. She brings Sarah a new sweater but it is too small. Debbie is embarrassed about this. Sarah serves the refreshments but the cake is too dry and the frosting tastes strange. Jack knocks over two pitchers of lemonade. They all decide it would be a great idea to go to a nearby ice cream parlor for some ice cream and cake.

Summary Chart: Promising

Type	*Sample sentence*	*Notes*
Statement	I'll be there at 8:00. I will call you. We'll have the money by Tuesday.	The future tense with "will" can stand alone as a promise. This is the most common form of promise.
	I promise I'll call you. I promise you that I'll call you.	
	I assure you that I'll call.	"I assure you" is more formal or used in writing.
	I give you my word that I'll come. I'll come. I give you my word. I'll come. You can count on me.	These types are commonly used informally.
	You can count on me to help. You can depend on me to help.	
	I swear I'll never tell anyone. I won't tell anyone. I swear.	"I swear" is a very strong promise.
	I guarantee this car will get 35 mpg.	Used for things and services.
"If" clause	We'll have the car ready by noon if all goes well.	The promise must be kept only if the condition is met.
	If you wash the dishes, I'll cook.	Notice the tenses: Condition—present tense Promise—future tense
Imperative	I'll be there. Count on it. Believe me. Trust me.	Used to emphasize that you are sincere, or to make the promise stronger.

Summary Chart: Apologizing

Parts of apology	*Sample sentence*	*Notes*
Regret/ Request	I'm really sorry. Please forgive me.	All the parts of an apology are not required. An apology may consist of one or more of these parts.
Excuse/ Reason	I didn't mean to do it. I was too busy to finish it.	
Promise	It won't happen again.	
Offer	I'll make it up to you. I'll buy you another one.	
Expressions of Acceptance of Apology	No problem. That's OK. I understand. Don't worry about it. Don't mention it. It doesn't matter.	

Summary Chart: Expressing Regret and Sympathizing

Type	*Sample sentences*	*Notes*
I'm sorry \ regret I regret /	I'm sorry I didn't take that class. I wish I had taken that class. I wish I hadn't taken that class.	Contrast with apology. In expressing regret, you are not apologizing to someone for something.
I'm sorry— sympathizing	I'm sorry (that) you didn't win. I'm sorry to hear you lost.	We sympathize with someone who has been hurt in some way or when something unpleasant has happened to someone.

UNIT 

EXPRESSING OPINIONS, AGREEING AND DISAGREEING

Expressing Opinions

An opinion is a statement of personal judgment about something or someone. There are two ways to do this.

I think it's going to rain. (Statement)	In my opinion, it's going to rain. (Use of a fixed expression)

STATEMENT

There are a number of verbs we commonly use to signal that a statement we are making is an opinion. This type of sentence may be used in informal as well as formal situations.

Listening In

Some family members are discussing whether or not to move to another house.

Mr. Reynolds: I think moving is the solution to our problem of space.

Mrs. Reynolds: Well, personally, I feel that this house is very comfortable. I don't think we really need the extra space at all.

Gary (son): It seems to me that we would be much happier in a house that had a big back yard.

Notice the verbs used in the dialogue to indicate that one is expressing an opinion.

I think . . . .
I feel . . . .
I don't think . . . .
It seems to me . . . .
I believe . . . .

The adverb "personally" is frequently used in spoken opinion statements. We can, of course, state our opinions without giving one of these signals to indicate that it is an opinion. These signals soften the statement. For example, if we read the first line of the dialogue without the special verb, it becomes stronger.

Moving is the solution to our problem of space.

Karen (daughter): I think moving would be fun.

Mrs. Reynolds: I'm sorry, but I still believe we're fine here. Besides, we can't afford to move.

Your Turn

Complete the following statements to express your opinion.

1. I ____________ that criminals should ____________.
2. Personally, I ____________ that homework ____________.
3. Pets ____________, I think.
4. ____________, taxes are too high.

FIXED EXPRESSIONS

Fixed expressions:
If you ask me . . . .
In my opinion . . . .

We often use certain fixed phrases when we want to make it clear we are expressing our opinion. By using these expressions, we emphasize the fact that the statements we make are our own ideas. For example, the earlier conversation among the members of the Reynolds family could be rephrased and they could use these fixed expressions.

Mr. Reynolds: If you ask me, moving is the solution to our problem of space.

Mrs. Reynolds: Well, in my opinion this house is very comfortable. I don't think we really need the extra space at all, etc.

Listening In

Two students are discussing a course they took together.

Ann: How did you like the chemistry course last semester?

Fred: If you ask me, the course could have been better organized.

Ann: I think you're right, Fred. In my opinion, he has taught that course so many times that he is bored with it and just doesn't care anymore.

Your Turn

A. Express your opinion about your school, university or institution.

1. If you ask me ______________ .
2. It seems to me that ______________ .
3. In my opinion, ______________ .

B. Choose a classmate to work with. Interview each other about a current issue or a controversial topic. Use a variety of phrases to signal your opinions.

Example:

You: What do you think about women fighting in the military?

Classmate: Personally, I feel fighting should be left to men.

You: Well, I think that if men have to fight, then women should, too.

Agreeing and Disagreeing

By agreeing with someone we express support for an opinion that s/he has expressed. Disagreeing means giving an opinion that is different from the one previously expressed. This support or lack of it can be expressed strongly or can be softened.

For example, if your friend says: "I think my brother is a wonderful tennis player," you can say:

You're right. (Direct Agreement)	I don't agree. (Direct Disagreement)

Or you can be less forceful and say:

Perhaps you're right. (Reluctant agreement)	I wish I could agree with you. (Softened disagreement)

DIRECT AGREEMENT

The following statements are commonly used to agree in either formal or informal situations:

I agree.
That's true.
That's right.
You're right.

Adverbs are also used frequently to show agreement.

Definitely.
Absolutely.
Naturally.
Of course.

Listening In

A. Some friends are discussing where to go on vacation.

Philip: I think the beach is the best place to go in August.

Rick: I agree. It will be much too hot anywhere else.

Joe: That's true. So, let's decide once and for all. We'll have the best time at Hunter's Beach, I think.

Rick: Definitely.

- Identify the expressions of agreement.

B. Friends are talking about the weather.

George: It sure is hot today.

Tim: I'll say!

Ben: But, it seems to me it's going to rain.

George: No doubt about it. The sky's getting darker every minute.

Many forms are used in informal agreement:

You can say that again.
You bet!
I'll say.
That's for sure.
Yeah.
No doubt about it.

C. Classmates are discussing summer school.

Ray: It's tough studying during the summer.

Bruce: Yeah, I know what you mean.

Ann: We could use a vacation right now.

Bill: That's for sure!

Your Turn

Complete the following exchanges by agreeing with the statement. Add a reason.

Example: It's important to eat breakfast./Definitely. We need energy in the morning.

1. Food is getting more expensive every day.
2. Our math teacher really makes us work.
3. I think long hair looks better on women than short hair.
4. The last reading test was easy.
5. Swimming is good exercise.

DIRECT DISAGREEMENT

Common forms for disagreeing are the negative forms of "agree."

I disagree.

I don't agree.

I don't think so.

A reason for the disagreement generally follows.

These forms are very straightforward and direct. They are commonly used with friends and family (and in debates). In more formal situations it is advisable to use more indirect forms (see the section on "Softened Disagreement.")

Listening In

A husband and wife are discussing a possible transfer to another city.

Husband: I think taking this new job would be a good idea.

Wife: I don't think so. We've lived here for ten years and we have a lot of nice friends in this city.

Husband: My job is more important than the neighbors we have.

Wife: I don't agree with you. I don't think you can even compare the two.

Your Turn

Disagree with the following statements. Use the direct forms and add a reason.

Example: Money is the cause of most divorces./I don't agree. There isn't any one cause for divorces.

1. English is more difficult than most other languages.
2. City life is much more exciting than life in the country.
3. The youngest child in the family is usually spoiled.
4. Most people in this town are unfriendly.

The following expressions are very informal. In formal situations they might be considered abrupt or rude.

You've got to be kidding/joking.
You must be kidding/joking.
That's ridiculous/absurd.
No way.
You can't really think that.
You can't be serious.
Not really.

Listening In

Two students are talking in the dormitory.

Jack: Summer is the best time to take courses.

Jim: You've got to be kidding. It's too hot to think.

Jack: That's ridiculous. Hot weather stimulates the brain. Besides, all the buildings are air conditioned.

Jim: No way! Only about a third of them are.

Your Turn

Disagree with each statement using informal forms. Add a reason.

1. Your roommate seems like a very serious student.
2. $250 is a good price for a new bicycle.
3. What a beautiful painting! Van Gogh is the best painter of all time.

RELUCTANT AGREEMENT

Sometimes we agree with something which we would rather not agree with. Often we are reluctant to agree because the situation is unpleasant. To show our hesitancy we might say:

I'm afraid I have to agree.

I'm afraid you're right.

I hate to admit it, but you're right.

I hate to say it, but I agree.

Perhaps you're right.

Listening In

A. Two friends are talking about a roommate.

Dan: It seems to me your roommate is very messy.

Paul: I hate to say it, but you're right.

Dan: Well, I guess you'll get used to it eventually.

Paul: I hope so!

- Why do you think Paul is reluctant to agree with Dan?

B. Two friends are talking about their apartment.

Karen: The roof has obviously been leaking. Look at that big crack.

Alice: I'm afraid you're right. We'd better call the landlord.

- Why do you think Alice says "I'm afraid you're right"?

C. Some friends are traveling together by car.

Carl: Check the map again. I think we're on the wrong road.

Sam: I hate to admit it, but you're right. We should have taken a left turn ten miles back.

Your Turn

Use the forms for reluctant agreement to respond to the following statements.

1. We need a new car this year.
2. She really doesn't look healthy.
3. You should quit smoking.
4. It looks like rain. We'll probably have to cancel the picnic.
5. Nancy looks very unhappy. She must have failed another quiz.
6. It's time to clean this house. It's a mess!
7. It looks like I'll have to repeat this course.

SOFTENED DISAGREEMENT

Often, we must disagree in a situation in which we do not feel we can be direct. If we want to be polite, or if we are trying to avoid an argument, or if we are talking to someone in a position of authority, it is safest to soften our disagreement.

We use certain phrases when we want to disagree very politely. We appear to agree at first, but the result is that we are in fact disagreeing.

I agree, but . . . .
That's true, but . . . .

Listening In

A. A student and his/her advisor are discussing courses.

Advisor: I think you should take another English class.

Student: I agree that my English isn't perfect, but I don't have time.

Advisor: You have an easy schedule in your other classes, so I think you'll have enough time.

Student: That's true, but I'm so tired of taking English.

B. Two acquaintances are discussing politics at a dinner party.

Ms. May: Taxes these days are outrageous. We shouldn't have to pay such high city taxes.

Mr. Sayle: I agree, but those taxes pay for a lot of services—street cleaning, garbage collection, transportation . . . .

Ms. May: You may have a point, but for the amount of taxes we pay you'd think the services would be better. My street is full of pot holes and the buses are always breaking down.

Mr. Sayle: Yes, well, I find the services quite adequate.

Ms. May: I wish I could agree with you.

Another way of softening disagreement is to acknowledge the other person's point of view before stating your disagreement.

You may have a point, but . . . .
I understand what you're saying, but . . . .
I see your point; however . . . .
Well, there are always two sides to every story.
I wish I could agree with you, but . . . .

Your Turn

Disagree politely in the following situations.

1. New York is the best place to live.
2. Football is the most exciting sport.
3. This textbook is too difficult for us.
4. Cats make the best pets.

SUMMING UP: AGREEING AND DISAGREEING

Your Turn

A. Make a statement of opinion about living in a foreign country using the structural cues given below. Then have another student respond by agreeing or disagreeing with your statement.

Example: If you ask me, food is generally a problem./I'm afraid you're right.

1. I believe ________________.
2. Personally, I feel ________________.
3. In my opinion, ________________.
4. I think ________________.
5. It seems to me that ________________.

B. Express your opinion about something to a classmate. The classmate will agree or disagree with you.

Example: The space program was a waste of money./You've got to be kidding. A lot of important technology was developed from it.

Role Play

Use a variety of forms for expressing opinions and agreeing/disagreeing.

Characters: Mr. Carson
Mrs. Carson

Mr. Carson and his wife are at home discussing the repainting of their apartment. He likes the color brown and his wife likes white. He prefers to hire professional painters and she wants to paint the apartment herself. He's afraid that his wife can't do the painting. She disagrees and promises that she'll do a good job. Finally they agree to do it themselves.

Summary Chart: Expressing Opinions

Type	*Sample sentence*	*Notes*
Statement	I think we should vote for him. believe ” ” feel ” ” It seems to me that it's better to paint it white.	These phrases signal that our opinion follows. We often use the adverb *personally* at the beginning of these statements. "Personally, I think we should vote for him."
Fixed expression	If you ask me, it's a terrible idea. To my mind, he has a good point there. In my opinion, we should cancel the order.	These expressions make it clear that we are expressing our personal opinion.

Summary Chart: Agreeing and Disagreeing

Type	*Sample sentence*	*Notes*
Direct agreement	I agree. You're right. That's true. That's right.	These statements may be used formally or informally.
	Definitely. Absolutely. Naturally. Of course.	These adverbs are commonly used to express agreement.
Direct disagreement	I disagree. I don't agree.	This is a straightforward way to express disagreement.
Reluctant agreement	I'm afraid I have to agree. I hate to admit it, but you're right. I hate to say it, but that's true.	We use these kinds of statements when we agree about something unpleasant or when we wish that we didn't agree.
Softened disagreement	That's true, but there's a better way. I agree, but I've noticed some problems there. You may have a point, but it's hard to believe those statistics. I wish I could agree with you, but I find it difficult to understand your point.	We use these kinds of statements to politely acknowledge another person's opinion while we are disagreeing.

UNIT **VI**

COMPLIMENTING, CONGRATULATING, CRITICIZING, AND COMPLAINING

Complimenting

To compliment means to say something positive about someone, something, or some place. It is polite to make a response to a compliment to show that you accept it.

There are three common and easy-to-learn ways to give compliments; (there are other possible ways). In this situation, your friend has a new car and you want to tell him that you like it.

Your new car is beautiful!/I really like your new car!/This is a very nice car.

In English, there are a number of things about which one can give a compliment:

1. a person's *physical appearance*
   You look wonderful./Did you go to Florida for the holidays?
2. a person's *attributes or abilities*
   I really enjoyed your speech. You did a good job./That was a very interesting paper you wrote. You write beautifully./You really have a green thumb.
3. *clothing*
   I like your tie./That's a beautiful dress./That color looks nice on you.
4. *accessories*
   I like your purse. Is it new?/Those are pretty earrings./That's a beautiful ring. Is it an antique?

Examine the list of things about which one can give a compliment.

Do these differ from those in your country? If so, explain how.

Are there any things which you *do* compliment people on in your culture which are not on the list?

5. *possessions*
   I like your fancy new car./That's a beautiful painting./Your stereo system sounds great.
6. *food*
   This soup is delicious./That cake smells wonderful./I really like your tuna casserole.
7. *environment*
   This is a great apartment. It's so big./I like the view from your window./I like the way you've decorated your house.

Listening In

The most common way to accept a compliment is to say "thanks."

To make the compliment stronger, "really" can be put in before the verb or the adjective; "so" or "very" can go before an adjective, and "such" can go before a noun phrase.

George: Hi, Mary! I like your new dress.
Mary: Thanks, I'm glad you like it.

Sonia: That's a nice jacket. Is it new?
Pat: No, I've had it for years. But thanks, anyway.

Chris: The dinner was delicious.
Jane: Thanks, I'm glad you enjoyed it. Let's get together again soon.

Linda: This is such a nice apartment. It's so sunny.
Debbie: Thanks. I'm really enjoying living here.

Your Turn

A. Practice giving compliments in all three ways; include the words to make the compliment stronger.
   1. Your house is ____________.

2. I ______________ like your ______________ .
3. ______________ beautiful picture.

B. Choose a partner. Complete the following dialogues, taking turns giving compliments and responding.
   1. a: That blouse (shirt/dress) looks ______________ .
      b: (Response)
   2. a: Those shoes ______________ . Are they new?
      b: (Response)
   3. a: This is a ______________ room.
      b: (Response)
   4. a: I ______________ your new ______________ .
      b: (Response)
   5. a: You're a ______________ .
      b: (Response)

American women (more commonly than men) often use the word "love" when they like something a great deal. Students from other cultures may find this use of the verb "love" strange or exaggerated. In some languages "love" is used only to show one's feelings for other people, while in the United States it's possible to "love" kinds of food ("I love spaghetti"), books, courses at school, articles of clothing, etc.

SUMMING UP: COMPLIMENTING

Your Turn

Compliment the following things. The teacher or classmate must respond appropriately. Refer to the dialogues. Use a variety of forms.

1. an attribute of your teacher
2. an ability of a classmate
3. a classmate's clothing
4. a classmate's possession
5. the environment
6. your teacher's appearance
7. a classmate's accessories
8. a classmate's physical appearance

Congratulating

Saying "Congratulations" means that you are expressing pleasure at the achievement or good fortune of another person.

Look at the following situation. Mary has just won first place in a swimming competition. Her friend Peter might say:

Congratulations! / Congratulations on such a great race! / Congratulations for winning first place!

Congratulations can be followed by:
on + Noun phrase
or
for + ing verb
Congratulations are not used for birthdays.

He might also add a comment such as:

I'm really proud of you.
I'm very happy for you.
You must be really proud of yourself.
I'll bet you're pleased.

Listening In

A. Friends are discussing the science fair.

Andrea: Guess what! I won the science award.

Pam: Congratulations! I'm really happy for you.

Andrea: Thanks. I really didn't think I'd get it.

B. Two friends meet on the street.

Jason: Hey, Mark! Congratulations on your promotion.

Mark: Thanks. I can sure use the raise in salary. And I hear you're getting married. Congratulations!

Jason: Thanks. Jennifer and I are getting married in April.

C. Some friends are talking in the school cafeteria.

Ali: Congratulations for getting an "A" on the test.

Carmen: Thank you. I really studied for that test. How are you doing?

Ali: I finally finished my research paper last night.

Carmen: Congratulations!

Ali: It was very hard work.

D. An employer and an employee meet in the office.

Mr. Wilson: Congratulations! I just heard that your wife had a baby.

Mr. Devlin: Yes, that's right. It's a girl! Her name is Alicia.

What are the congratulations for in all of these dialogues?

What is the most common way of responding to a congratulation?

When do people in your country congratulate each other?

How do they respond?

Your Turn

Each student tells the class about some achievement or good luck they have had recently. The other students practice congratulating. Use a variety of forms.

Criticizing

Criticizing means making a negative judgment about someone or something. Thus, it is the opposite of complimenting, which means making a positive judgment. Criticizing stresses faults, while complimenting stresses merits.

While it is easy and enjoyable to compliment, it is sometimes more difficult to criticize without being rude or hurting someone's feelings. There are several ways in which we can criticize, or even avoid criticizing. Look at the following situation and the possible responses. Gary is considering renting an apartment. He takes Marsha, a friend, to look at it and asks for her opinion. Marsha thinks that it is very depressing because there are few windows and the walls are painted dark brown.

Gary: Well, what do you think?

Marsha:	It's very depressing. I wouldn't want to live here.	It's in a good location. I wonder if the landlord would let you repaint the walls a lighter color so it would be brighter.	Well . . . is it expensive?
	(Direct criticism)	(Indirect criticism)	(Avoiding open criticism)

Notice that in the first alternative, Marsha directly states her criticism. In the second, she makes a positive statement and states her criticism indirectly. In the third, she avoids criticizing by changing the subject.

DIRECT CRITICISM

In certain situations it is acceptable to criticize someone or something by stating your opinion in a straightforward way. This type of criticism is commonly used to criticize public figures or persons not present, or the actions of persons under one's supervision or authority or things which have no personal significance to the listener.

Listening In

A. Two friends are leaving a movie.

George: That was a lousy ending.

Sam: Yeah. I thought they would explain more of what happened earlier in the film.

B. Two friends are in the school cafeteria.

Joyce: This coffee is awful.

Wendy: I never buy it anymore. It always tastes like dish water.

- Why does Joyce feel free to criticize the coffee? Do you think she would make the same comment if she were drinking coffee which Wendy had made?

We freely criticize things such as books, television programs, movies, the weather or food in restaurants. We feel free to criticize because none of these things are normally associated with someone's personal feelings. Therefore, there is no danger of being rude or hurting anyone's feelings.

C. Two roommates are watching TV.

Joy: We really need to get this TV repaired.

Helen: I know. The color is terrible and we can't get channel 8 anymore.

- Who do you think the TV belongs to? Why?

D. Two friends are talking.

Barry: This weather is miserable. I hate rain.

Sarah: Me, too. I haven't been able to play tennis for weeks.

Your Turn

Each student thinks of several things which he/she has negative opinions about which may be freely criticized in a direct manner. In pairs, one student criticizes something and another either agrees or disagrees with the criticism.

Listening In

A. Two friends are discussing current events.

Jeff: Did you hear that the mayor wants to raise the subway fares again?

Jane: Yes. The paper says that in the long run that will hurt the city because people will start driving their cars again and pollute the air.

Jeff: I heard he wants to raise taxes, too, to pay for the new school they're building. I can tell you one thing, I won't vote for him again next year.

Jane: Me either!

Newspapers, magazines, and the general public freely criticize public figures such as politicians, writers, actors or musicians and their policies or actions.

B. Two classmates are talking.

Henry: Mr. Taylor's class is really boring.

Will: I know what you mean. I'll bet he's given the same lectures for the last twenty years.

We sometimes criticize people who are not present very bluntly. It would be very rude to say the same thing directly to the person in question.

C. A teacher and student are talking.

In some situations it is one's job or role to judge the actions or work of others. In such situations, it is not considered rude to use direct statements.

Teacher: Ali, this paper is very poorly written. You'll have to rewrite it. Please spend a little more time checking your spelling and grammar this time.

Ali: OK. I'm sorry. I was studying for a math test and I wrote it in a hurry. I'll do better next time.

Teacher: I hope so. I know you usually put more effort into your work.

- Why does the teacher feel free to directly criticize Ali's work?

D. An employer is criticizing his employee.

The employer criticizes his secretary's typing speed and then, to soften the criticism, suggests a way for her to improve. This makes the criticism helpful.

Employer: Your typing is not adequate for this job. I've talked to the head of the office and she has agreed to allow you to take time off to take a typing course.

There are several things to keep in mind when criticizing someone's behavior:

1. Always consider the feelings of the person being criticized.
2. Be specific about the behavior which is being criticized. General, vague criticisms are rarely helpful. Criticize the behavior, not the person.
3. Criticize only those things which the person is able to change.
4. Be sure your criticism is constructive. That is, be sure that you are criticizing something which it would be useful for the person to be aware of.

E. The same employer criticizing his employee.

Employer: You didn't finish the report that needed to be typed last night.

Employee: I'm sorry, but you know that I have three children and I can't stay late to type. You didn't give me the report until nearly 5:00.

Employer: You're so stupid. Why can't you be as good a secretary as Mrs. Oakes?

- Why is Dialogue D appropriate but Dialogue E not appropriate?
- What is wrong with Dialogue E?

INDIRECT OR SOFTENED CRITICISM

There are several ways in which we can make criticism indirect or soften it in order to be more polite and considerate of the other person's feelings.

1. State your criticism in the form of a question. (This allows the listener to explain or justify his/her behavior.) Use polite question forms such as "Would you mind . . . ." or "Would you please . . . ."

2. Make your criticism less direct by using tentative language such as "I think . . . .", "Perhaps . . . .", or "I'm not sure, but . . . ."
3. Add a positive remark or compliment to your criticism.
4. Include advice for improving along with your criticism.

Listening In

A. Two friends are shopping. Susan does not like the dress Mary has chosen.

Mary: Should I buy this dress?

Susan: It's a nice dress, but I don't think the color suits you.

B. Two friends are talking.

George: What do you think of this cake? It's the first time I've ever baked one. I'm practicing for my mother's birthday.

Sally: The cake is really moist and delicious, but I think the frosting is a little too sweet. I'd use less sugar next time.

C. Two roommates are talking.

Bill: How do I look?

Tim: Are you sure you want to wear that green tie with your blue suit? The brown one might look better.

D. Two friends are talking. Tina has asked Gail to read her composition.

Tina: Well, what do you think?

Gail: The content is very interesting, but if I were you I'd check the spelling of some of the words before handing it in.

E. A student believes that his teacher has made a mistake in correcting his test.

Ned: Mr. Brown, would you please explain to me why you've marked this question wrong. I can't seem to find the mistake.

Certain things we can criticize directly; however, if the thing to be criticized has some sort of personal importance to the hearer, it is best to criticize more indirectly, or soften the criticism. For example, in Dialogue A, Mary has chosen the dress herself. In Dialogue B, the cake is important to George because he baked it.

Notice that in these dialogues each person asked for the other's opinion; therefore, the friend felt free to criticize, but in each case did it politely. In each situation the person was capable of changing the thing being criticized. (Mary could choose a different dress if she agreed with Susan. George could use less sugar the next time.)

It is especially important to be tactful when criticizing someone in a position of authority such as a teacher or supervisor. It is usually considered rude to criticize directly.

Mr. Brown: Let me see . . . . I'm sorry, I must have made a mistake. Your answer is correct. Let me give you the extra points.

OR

Ned might also have said:

Ned: Mr. Brown, could you tell me why this answer is wrong?

OR

Ned: Mr. Brown, would you mind re-checking this answer?

- How do you think the teacher might have responded if Ned had said:

Ned: You're wrong, Mr. Brown. My answer is right.

Your Turn

How have the speakers in Dialogues A–E softened their criticisms? For each situation, soften the criticism in a *different* way.

Example: In Dialogue A, Susan could have softened her criticism by using a question.

Susan: Do you think that's the right color for you?

Don't be confused. If the words "interesting, unusual or different" are used to describe such things as books, movies, television programs, courses or jobs, they may truly be positive statements. They are only neutral when applied to objects which would normally be complimented in a more direct and obvious way.

AVOIDING OPEN CRITICISM

In some situations, we may have a negative opinion, but we would prefer not to state it, either for fear of being rude, or because we do not want to hurt the other person's feelings. There are several ways in which people avoid stating their criticism when asked for an opinion.

1. Avoid stating a negative opinion by commenting on something which is related, but not exactly what you were asked to comment on.
   (Look back at the beginning of this section. Marsha avoids stating her true opinion that the apartment is depressing by asking if it is expensive. In other words, she changes the subject.)
2. Make a neutral or noncommittal statement.
   (When asked for an opinion, if one does not give an obviously positive opinion, the listener can guess that the opinion is probably negative.)

Listening In

A. Two friends are talking. Betty has just bought a new hat. Susan doesn't like it.

Betty: How do you like my new hat?

Susan: It's unusual. Where did you buy it?

B. Jack has brought his friend Sonia to a party. He obviously likes her very much. Although Paul has only just met her, he does not particularly like her.

Jack: Well, what do you think of Sonia? Isn't she great?

Paul: Well . . . she seems nice, but I really haven't had a chance to talk to her very much. Where did you meet her?

- What do you think Paul might have said if he had really liked Sonia?

Note, Susan uses the noncommittal word "unusual" to avoid having to lie by saying she likes the hat or hurting Betty's feelings by saying she doesn't like it. She knows that Betty must like the hat because she has already bought it; therefore, it would not be useful to tell Betty that the hat looks terrible on her.

Paul is placed in a position of having to state an opinion because he is asked, although he would prefer not to. He tries to avoid hurting Jack's feelings by making a neutral statement ("She seems nice") and then changing the subject. His use of "well . . ." to hesitate is also a signal that he does not feel very positive.

What's Happening?

1. What did the little girl say that hurt her grandmother's feelings?
2. Do you think the grandmother felt better after the little girl said, "I'm sorry your hat looks dumb"?
3. What could the little girl have said to hide her negative opinion about the hat?

what 'dya = what do you
good-looking = attractive
coat = jacket
fish for a compliment = ask for a compliment
loud = bright

Are there situations in your own culture where you would want to avoid or hide your criticism?

How would you hide your criticism in your language?

In your culture, would it be acceptable to tell a lie if someone asked your opinion and you didn't want to give a negative judgment?

1. Do you think Burt was sincere in complimenting Mike on his coat, or was he really fishing for a compliment?
2. How did Mike make it clear that he did not like Burt's coat?
3. What would you have said if you had thought Burt's coat was too loud?

SUMMING UP: CRITICIZING

Appropriate Responses

For each situation there are several possible responses listed. Discuss each response. Which response is the most direct? Which would be the most polite? Why? Are there any which would be inappropriate? Why? Which would be the most helpful? Why?

1. Your friend is playing a new record he has just bought. You don't particularly like it. He asks you what you think of it.
   a) It's OK, but I really don't care much for rock music myself.
   b) It just sounds like noise to me. How can you call that music?
   c) I think I prefer the classical music you were playing earlier.
   d) It's different. Who are the musicians?

2. One of your classmates has just given an oral report. The class is discussing the report and the teacher asks you to give your opinion of the report.
   a) It was lousy. His pronunciation is so bad that I couldn't understand half of it.
   b) The topic was very interesting and the photographs he showed helped us to imagine the countryside, but I think perhaps he needs to work on improving his pronunciation. I didn't understand everything.
   c) He should get an F, in my opinion.
   d) It was different.

3. Your roommate has made sandwiches for lunch. She didn't put any mayonnaise on them and they taste very dry.
   a) Thanks for making lunch. I think I'll put a little mayonnaise on mine. It's a little dry.
   b) Yuk! These sandwiches are too dry. Why didn't you put any mayonnaise on them?
   c) Don't you think these would be better with a little mayo? I'll get some.
   d) These sandwiches are good, but they'd be even better with a little mayonnaise!

Role Plays

Working with a partner, prepare short dialogues for the following situations.

1. In each situation criticize directly.
   a) You and your friend have just seen a movie. You didn't like it.
   b) Two friends are talking. A third friend has just bought a new car. You don't like it.
   c) You and your friends are discussing the food in the cafeteria.

2. In each situation, criticize, but do so indirectly.
   a) You are worried because your friend is not studying enough. You feel you must tell him.
   b) Tell your friend that she is talking too loud and disturbing other people in the library.
   c) Tell your classmate not to talk so much during class. You've noticed that the teacher and the other students seem annoyed.

3. In each situation, make a criticism, but add a positive remark to soften it.
   a) Your roommate has bought a new pair of shoes and asks your opinion of them.
   b) Your friend drives up in a new car and asks what you think of it.
   c) Your classmate has written a poem and asks what you think of it.

4. In each situation, avoid criticizing, although you have a negative opinion.
   a) Your friend asks you how you like his new shirt.
   b) A classmate has just finished a drawing and asks you what you think of it.
   c) Your teacher asks you whether you enjoyed the field trip.
   d) Your employer wants to rearrange the office and asks you whether you like the idea.

Complaining

Complaints are appropriate in a variety of circumstances. When we complain, often we are hoping to receive *sympathy or agreement.* In certain situations, we know that the person to whom we are complaining cannot do anything to change or improve the situation.

Sometimes we complain because we hope to receive *advice.*

At other times we complain simply to *make conversation.* Complaints can be used to "break the ice" with strangers.

Usually when we complain about a service or product to the business involved, it is because we expect the business to *do something to correct the situation* we are complaining about. Thus, most consumer complaints are for this purpose. We may also complain to individuals because we want them to do something to improve or correct the situation. Complaints often include criticisms.

I hate rain!	I feel lousy.	I'd like to return this iron.
(Discontent or dissatisfaction)	(Discomfort or pain)	(Consumer Complaint)

Our reasons for expressing these feelings may vary. In the following dialogues, you will find examples of different reasons for complaining.

DISCONTENT OR DISSATISFACTION

Very often we complain to our friends when we are unhappy.

Listening In

A. Two friends are talking.

Barry: This weather is miserable. I hate rain.

Susan: Me, too. I haven't been able to play tennis for weeks.

- What is Barry's reason for complaining? Does he want advice or sympathy, or is he just making conversation?

Do you remember the dialogue between Barry and Susan in the criticizing section? They both express negative judgments about the recent weather. Then Susan expresses her dissatisfaction at not being able to play tennis. You can see that complaints and criticisms are often expressed together.

Sometimes the distinction between a complaint and a criticism is unclear; sometimes it is not; do not worry about which is which.

B. Sid wonders why his coworker, Joe, looks so unhappy after talking to the boss.

Sid: Hey, what happened in there?

Joe: The boss just informed me that he needs the financial report on the Johnson account by 8:00 tomorrow morning. I'll have to work late and I have two tickets to the game tonight. There's no way I can get it done in time to go to the game.

Sid: Bad luck! It's going to be a great game, too.

From the context, can you guess what "go to waste" and "slaving away" mean?

Joe: Listen, why don't you take the tickets? There's no reason they should go to waste.

Sid: Well, I'll try not to feel too guilty knowing that you're slaving away while I'm enjoying the game. Maybe we can get tickets for the playoffs.

- Why does Joe complain? What does he expect from his coworker, Sid?
- Is Sid sympathetic to Joe's situation?
- How do you know? What expression does Sid use?
- If you were Joe, how would you feel about taking the tickets? Would you accept them?

"gee" is an exclamation similar to "wow" or "gosh."

"I'll say" is an informal expression of agreement.

In your country, do you ever use a complaint to start a conversation? Give an example of a situation where this might happen, if you think it might.

In the United States, typical subjects which people complain about to people they don't know are the weather, having to wait in long lines or for elevators, and traffic (especially in large cities). Do you have any similar situations in which people might complain in your country?

C. Two people who don't know each other are waiting for the bus on a cold morning.

a: Gee, it sure is cold this morning.

b: I'll say. The bus always seems to come late on cold mornings.

a: Yeah, I know what you mean. Do you usually catch the J13?

b: No, I usually catch a later bus, but I have a paper to write and I thought I'd get to the library early.

a: Oh, are you a student at Simmons College?

b: No, I go to the City University.

a: Really? My son graduated from there last year.

. . . (the conversation continues) . . .

- What is "a" complaining about.
- What do you think is the reason that "a" expresses this complaint to "b"?
- What is the result of "a"'s complaint?

D. George and Sally have just finished taking a final exam.

George: That test was really hard. I read all of the chapters he assigned, but I know I didn't do well.

Sally: I agree! That question about monopoly was unfair. He never even discussed that in class.

George: I think we should complain to the head of the department. If I fail this course, I'll probably lose my scholarship.

Sally: I think we should talk to the professor first. It only seems fair to give him a chance before we go over his head.

George: OK. Let's make an appointment to see him, and if he won't agree to forget that question then we'll talk to the head of the department.

- What do you think is George's purpose in complaining to Sally? What does he want her to do?
- What suggestion does George make? Do you think that's a good idea? Would you do the same thing?

Notice that in dialogues A, B, C, and D, a declarative statement was used to express the complaint.

A: This weather is miserable.
B: I'll have to work late.
C: It sure is cold this morning.
D: That test was really hard.

In many cases, when you are hoping that another person will agree with your complaint, you may use an interrogative or a tag question. For example,

A: This weather is miserable, isn't it?
(Isn't this weather miserable?)
B: (no change)
C: It sure is cold this morning, isn't it?

How could you change D to a question?

Your Turn

Each student makes a complaint about something with which s/he is discontented or dissatisfied. Use declarative sentences, or interrogatives or tag questions.

DISCOMFORT OR PAIN

We sometimes complain when we don't feel well, but usually only to close friends or to medical people. It is usually not considered polite to complain about discomfort or illness to strangers.

Listening In

A. Maryanne meets her friend Pete on the way to work.

Maryanne: Hi, Pete. How's it going?

Pete: To tell you the truth, I feel lousy. I think I'm coming down with the flu.

"I feel lousy" is a very informal way of saying that you don't feel well.

Maryanne: You should be home in bed.

Pete: I know, but I have a project report due tomorrow and I have to finish typing it.

Maryanne: Listen, I'm not too busy right now. Let's talk to the boss. If she agrees, I'll type it and you can go home and get some rest.

Pete: I'd really appreciate that.

There is an expression in English, "Misery loves company." Can you guess what it means? How does it relate to complaining?

1. Why does Pete feel free to complain to Maryanne?
2. What do you think Pete hopes to gain by complaining to her? Do you think he expects her to offer to help him?

B. Two days later Pete calls his doctor. The receptionist answers the phone.

Pete: I'd like to make an appointment to see Dr. Harris.

Recep.: Is this for a routine checkup?

Pete: No, I haven't been feeling well.

Recep.: What are your symptoms?

Pete: I've been running a fever of 102° since yesterday and I have a terrible headache.

Recep.: It sounds like you might have the flu. There's a lot of that going around. Dr. Harris's schedule is quite full, but if you come in at about two o'clock I'll see if she can fit you in.

"There's a lot of that going around" means that a lot of people have the flu at this time.

Pete: Thank you. I'll be there at two o'clock.

- What is Pete complaining about?
- What is his purpose in complaining? Is it the same as in dialogue A?
- When Pete describes how he feels, how does his language differ from when he was talking to Maryanne? Why?

C. Two friends are shopping.

Sarah: Ouch! These shoes are killing me!

Marge: They look very comfortable.

Sarah: Yeah. That's why I bought them, but the right one really pinches my toes.

Marge: Why don't we sit down and have something to drink?

Sarah: Great idea!

Marge: You know, we could stop at the shoe store on the way home. Sometimes they can stretch shoes for you.

- What is Sarah complaining about?
- What do you think she wants Marge to do?
- What suggestions/advice does Marge give?

Your Turn

Working in pairs, one student makes a complaint about physical discomfort or pain, and the other student makes an appropriate response. Remember that when Greetings were dealt with, the question "How are you?" was not answered with a true statement of feelings unless a friend is really asking specifically about one's state of health.

CONSUMER COMPLAINTS

A consumer is a person who buys a product or a service. If the product or service is unsatisfactory, then it is appropriate to complain to the business involved. In consumer complaints, the reason for complaining is always that we want the business *to do something to correct the situation.* As you will see from the dialogues, there are a variety of situations where it is appropriate to complain.

Keep the following points in mind when you make a consumer complaint. They will help you to receive a satisfactory response.

1. *State your complaint briefly and clearly.* Avoid being emotional. State the facts. Be firm, but polite.

   Example: This jacket has a broken zipper.
   This clock doesn't keep the correct time.

   You do not need to be apologetic. If you have paid for a product or service, you have the right to expect satisfaction. On the other hand, normally there is no need to be rude or aggressive. Most reputable businesses will try to correct the problem or replace the product, or do what is necessary to satisfy the customer.

2. State clearly exactly *what you want the business to do to correct the problem.*

   Example: I'd like to exchange it.
   I'd like you to replace it.
   I'd like a fresh cup of coffee.
   I'd like you to cancel this charge on my bill.

3. *Be sure you are talking to the person who can help you.* In some cases, a waiter or waitress or a salesperson may not have the authority to make the adjustment you wish. They may say something like, "I'm sorry, but there's nothing I can do" or "We can't give you a refund without a receipt." If you are not satisfied, ask to talk with the manager. In some stores there is a special department called the Complaint Department which you can go to with your problem.

Listening In

A. In a restaurant.

Customer: Excuse me, waiter. This soup isn't hot.

Waiter: I'm very sorry. I'll bring you a fresh bowl right away.

Customer: Thank you.

- Do you think the customer and the waiter were polite in this situation?
- What would happen in a similar situation in your country?

B. In a department store.

Salesperson: May I help you?

Customer: Yes, I'd like to return this iron.

Salesperson: What's wrong with it?

Customer: When I plug it in, nothing happens. It doesn't heat up.

Salesperson: Do you have the receipt?

Customer: Yes. Here it is.

Salesperson: This receipt says you bought this two months ago. I can't give you a refund after fourteen days, but I can send this to the factory for repairs.

- What did the customer want the salesperson to do?
- Why couldn't the salesperson do that?
- What did the salesperson offer to do instead?

Avoiding consumer problems:
As a consumer, there are a number of things which you can do to avoid problems:

1. Before buying anything, examine it carefully. If it is a piece of clothing, be sure to try it on. Check to see that there are no missing buttons or rips in the seams. If it is an electrical applicance or anything with moving parts, ask the salesperson to test it for you in the store.
2. Always save your receipt until you are sure that you are satisfied with the product.
3. Be sure that you understand the store's return, refund or exchange policies.
4. Find out if the product has any type of warranty or guarantee. Be sure you understand it.
5. If you are buying a service such as car repair, carpet cleaning or plumbing repair, ask for an estimate before the work is done. Get all agreements in writing to protect yourself.

C. Nancy took her typewriter to the repair shop to be cleaned and oiled because several of the keys were sticking. She paid \$42.00. After two weeks the keys began sticking again, so she took it back a second time. When she went to pick it up they gave her a bill for \$23.00.

Nancy: I don't understand this charge. I already paid \$42.00 to have the same problem fixed two weeks ago.

Salesperson: I'm sorry, but the \$23.00 is for labor. The repairman worked on it for an hour.

Nancy: I don't think I should have to pay twice to have the same problem fixed. I'd like to talk with the manager, please.

Salesperson: Well, all right.

(Nancy explains the situation again to the manager.)

Manager: I'm sorry for this misunderstanding. Of course there will be no additional charge.

- What is Nancy complaining about?
- Do you think Nancy was satisfied with the manager's response?

Your Turn

Working in pairs, develop short dialogues between a customer and a clerk, or between a customer and a store manager.

Listening In

John is complaining to his landlord. He calls him on the phone to discuss the heat in his apartment.

John: I'm having some problems with the heat in my unit.

Landlord: What exactly is the problem?

John: Well, the bedroom only gets up to about 50°, but the living room and the dining room are about 78°.

Landlord: Did you check it with a thermometer?

John: Yes. It's been like this for about a week now.

Landlord: OK. I'll have a look at it. Will you be home about 5:30 today?

John: Yes, I can be there by then. Thank you very much.

- What is John's complaint?
- What does he want the landlord to do?

Your Turn

Working in pairs, develop complaints between a tenant and a landlord or landlady.

SUMMING UP: CRITICIZING AND COMPLAINING

Listening In

Two roommates are talking.

Will: Darn it!

Herb: What's the matter?

Will: All day long I've been thinking about eating that last piece of cake and now it's gone.

Herb: Sorry. I ate it when I got home. Have some ice cream instead.

Will: You ate all the ice cream two days ago. No matter how much I buy, you always eat everything.

Herb: Stop complaining and eat some fruit or something. It's better for you anyway.

Will: I know, but I don't feel like eating anything that's good for me.

- Identify the criticisms and complaints in the dialogue.
- What other language functions can you find? (requests, apologies, suggestions or advice, commands, etc.)

Appropriate Responses

For each situation there are several possible responses listed. Discuss each response. Are there certain responses which are too direct or too indirect? Which one(s) do you think would be inappropriate? Which would be appropriate? Why? What other responses could you make?

1. You are in a restaurant. You have just added cream to your coffee and the cream is spoiled. You get the waiter's attention and you say:
   a) Excuse me, sir. This cream is spoiled. I'd like a fresh cup of coffee and a new pitcher of cream.
   b) I'm terribly sorry to bother you. I feel terrible about this. I didn't know that the cream was spoiled and I put some in my coffee. I'll be happy to pay for another cup of coffee.
   c) Hey! What kind of restaurant is this? Do you always give your customers spoiled cream? Bring me a fresh cup right away or I won't pay my bill.
2. You bought a clock two weeks ago which gains ten minutes a day. You want to exchange it for a new one. You take it back to the store and say:
   a) This is a lousy clock. How can you sell such junk? I want a new one.
   b) I'm so sorry to bother you with my problem, but this clock which I bought doesn't seem to work properly. Maybe I don't know how to set it properly, but it gains ten minutes a day. Would it be possible to exchange it for a new one if it isn't too much trouble for you?
   c) I'd like to exchange this clock. Here's the receipt. I've tried it for a week and it gains ten minutes a day.

Your Turn

A. Do you know what each of the following policies means? Discuss them with your teacher if you have questions.

   1. All sales are final.

2. Refunds with receipt only.
3. Exchanges will be made only within seven days of purchase.
4. No refunds. Exchanges only.
5. We guarantee all parts installed by us for 90 days after date of repair, but do not guarantee other parts in your set. (From a TV repair shop.)
6. We guarantee all parts and labor for 30 days.
7. All parts are under manufacturer's warranty for 1 year from date of purchase with receipt.

B. Make an appropriate complaint to the person involved in each situation. Then discuss what your purpose for complaining is in each situation and how you think the other person might respond.

Example: The temperature is 100° today. You and your friend are standing waiting for a bus.

It sure is hot, isn't it? OR The heat really bothers me.

1. Your classmate has borrowed your book without your permission. Complain to him/her when you see him/her the next day.
2. Your roommate wakes up at 3:00 a.m. to ask you a question about his/her math assignment.
3. Your sister forgot your birthday. Complain to a friend.
4. Your next-door neighbor is having a party. Complain to your roommate about the noise.
5. Complain to your neighbor about the noise.
6. You and another person are waiting for the elevator. Complain about how slow the elevator is.

Role Play

A. Choose a partner. Prepare dialogues for each situation. (Minimum 4 to 6 exchanges.)

1. You are talking to a friend who always seems very calm and relaxed. You always feel very nervous and rushed. Complain about your feelings and try to get some advice.
2. Complain to your doctor that you always feel nervous and tired.
3. The telephone company has sent you a bill for $396 dollars worth of long distance calls to Uruguay. You don't even know anyone in Uruguay.
4. You and a friend are eating in a restaurant. You are in a hurry to get to a movie and the service is very slow. First you complain to your friend, and then to the waiter/waitress.

B. Choose a partner and select one of the situations below. Prepare a short role play and then act it out for the class.

1. Two friends are at Tim's house discussing plans for a picnic. They *disagree* on where to have the picnic and what to take along to eat and for entertainment. After they have expressed *their opinions* at length, they finally *agree.* Sharon *compliments* Tim on his grill but *criticizes* his picnic basket. They notice that the weather is changing for the worse and begin to *complain.* They discuss whether they should cancel the picnic. A decision is finally made and they . . . . (you decide the ending).

2. Two friends are discussing their math class. They have *different opinions* about the teacher, the amount of homework, the tests and the other students in the class. They *agree* about certain points and *disagree* about others. They *compliment* the professor for ______________ but they *criticize* him for ______________ and they *complain* to each other. They decide that overall the class is a good/bad one.

Summary Chart: Complimenting

Three sentence types for compliments

I. *Noun/Noun Phrase*	+ *Linking Verb*	+ *(Intensifier)**	+ *Adjective*
That dress	looks	very	nice
The chicken	is	so	delicious.
Your English	sounds	very	good.
This chair	feels	really	comfortable.
That cake	smells		wonderful.

II. *Pronoun*	+ *(Intensifier)*	+ *Verb*	+ *Noun Phrase*
I		enjoyed	your speech.
I		like	your sweater.
I	(really)	love	your new apartment.
I		enjoyed	the party.
I		like	the way you dance.

III. *Noun/Pronoun*	+ *(Intensifier)*	+ *BE*	+ *(Intensifier)*	+ *Adjective*	+ *Noun Phrase*
You		are	such	a good	cook.
This		is		a nice	apartment.
That	(really)	is		a pretty	color.
Those		are		beautiful	earrings.
Your son		is	really	a handsome	boy.

* The parentheses mean that the item is optional.

Summary Chart: Congratulating

Congratulations!		+ many possible phrases:
	+ on + such a great race. (Noun Phrase)	I'm really proud of you. I'm very happy for you.
	+ for + winning first place. (-ing Verb Phrase)	You must be very proud of yourself. I'll bet you're pleased.

Most common response: Thanks!

Summary Chart: Criticizing

Type	*Sample sentence*	*Notes*
Direct Criticism of:		
Things	That was a lousy movie. This book is boring.	It is acceptable to directly criticize things which have no particular personal attachment to the listener.
Public Figures & others not present	The President's foreign policy is a big mistake. Mrs. Brown gave us too much work to do.	It is common to directly criticize people not present since there is no danger of hurting anyone's feelings. (Caution: No one enjoys hearing someone complain constantly or gossip.)
Those under one's supervision or authority	Boss: This letter is too messy to send. You'll have to retype it. Mother: Your posture is awful. stand up straight.	
Indirect or Softened Criticism of:		There are several ways to ensure politeness: 1. State your criticism in the form of a question. 2. Use tentative language. 3. Make a positive remark in addition to the criticism. 4. Include advice with your criticism.
People in Authority	Employee to Boss: Do you think perhaps we could change the way we keep track of our expenses?	
Friends or Acquaintances	That coat looks warm, but I don't think the style is right for you. Your handwriting is very hard to read. Why don't you do these practice exercises?	

Summary Chart: Criticizing (Continued)

Type	*Sample sentence*	*Notes*
Avoiding Open Criticism	Joe: How do you like my tie? Bill: Well, it's different. Sue: Do you like my hat? Bob: It's interesting. Sam: What do you think of this music? Jeff: I really haven't been paying attention.	In certain situations you may have a negative opinion, but do not wish to express it.

Summary Chart: Complaining

Type	*Sample sentences*	*Notes*
Personal		
— expressing discontent or dissatis-faction	I hate this course I'm taking. I don't have time for anything else. The boss doesn't give us enough time for lunch. I'm going to get an ulcer from eating too fast. The weather's been terrible lately.	We often complain to receive sym-pathy or agreement or advice from someone. We also complain simply to make conversation.
— expressing discomfort or pain	These shoes are so uncomfortable. I feel lousy. I think I'm getting a cold.	
Consumer	This coat has a stain on the sleeve. I noticed it as soon as I got home. I'd like to exchange it, please.	We complain if we are not satisfied with a product or service and we wish to correct the problem. State the problem, then state what you would like done to rectify the problem.

REVIEW ROLE PLAYS

The Reception

Greeting people and making introductions.

Characters: You
A new student
Classmates (any number)
Faculty members (any number)

Your university/school is having a beginning-of-the-year reception to welcome faculty and students. You notice a person standing in the corner of the room all alone. You decide to go up to him/her and *introduce* yourself. He/she in turn *introduces* himself/herself to you. You see some old classmates and you *greet* them with enthusiasm. You *introduce* them to your new friend. Since he/she is a new student, you offer to introduce him/her to some of the faculty members that you know. First, you *introduce* the head of the English Department, then the foreign student advisor, and next the head of the athletic department. (You may add more faculty members if you wish.)

An Eventful Trip by Plane

Requesting, advising, complaining, criticizing, apologizing, and promising

Characters: Mr. Wright
Mrs. Wright, his wife
an airline steward (or stewardess)
airline employee at pick-up station (baggage claim area)
airline office employee

Mr. and Mrs. Wright are on a plane flying from Seattle to San Francisco. They are very demanding during this short flight. They *request* water from the steward. They *ask* what time it is and they *want to know* if the plane will be arriving on time. They *ask about* the present weather conditions in San Francisco. They *complain* that there is no soap in the lavatory. Mrs. Wright *complains* that the airplane is very cold and she *requests* a couple of blankets. The steward is very patient and very polite.

The plane finally lands in San Francisco and Mr. and Mrs. Wright deplane. They follow the other passengers to the baggage claim area. The time slowly goes by and they have not seen any of their three suitcases. Mr. Wright *criticizes* the airport crew for lack of efficiency. Mrs. Wright *criticizes* the airline for causing inconvenience to the passengers. Finally, Mr. Wright *complains* to one of the employees at the baggage claim station. He *apologizes* for the delay but *advises* Mr. Wright to wait a little longer because all of the luggage is not yet out. But when all of the luggage is out, the Wrights do not see theirs so they go to the airline office *to complain* to the employee there. He *apologizes* and *promises* to send their luggage to their hotel as soon as it arrives.

The Research Paper

Greeting people, advising, cautioning, promising, criticizing, complaining, apologizing, and requesting.

Characters: Bob
Dave

Bob hasn't begun to work on his research paper yet. The paper is due in a few days. His friend Dave has helped him in the past, so Bob decides to get help from him.

Bob finds Dave in the cafeteria and they *greet* each other. Without wasting any time, Bob *asks* Dave to help him to organize his research paper. Dave *advises* Bob to buy one of those "How to Write a Research Paper" books, but Bob *complains* that those books never really help very much. Dave indirectly *criticizes* Bob for always waiting until the last minute to do his assignments. He cautions Bob that their engineering professor never accepts late papers. Bob *apologizes* for always asking Dave to help him, but he repeats his *request* for help. He tries *complimenting* Dave on his intelligence in order to make him more receptive. Dave doesn't respond favorably to Bob's compliments, but instead he directly *criticizes* his laziness. Bob *promises* that this will be the last time that he'll ask for help. Dave finally gives in and starts to give Bob some *advice* on how to write his research paper.

Intruders in the Apartment

Greeting people, introducing, saying good-bye, requesting, commanding, advising, cautioning, sympathizing, expressing regret, and promising

Characters: Debbie
Barbara
Two police officers

Debbie and Barbara are university students who share an apartment on campus. Before leaving for her evening class, Debbie forgot to lock the door, and when Barbara gets home, she finds the door ajar. All the closets and drawers have been opened and the stereo and television are gone.

Debbie comes back from her class and *greets* Barbara. Then she notices the state of the apartment. Barbara *tells* her to come in quickly and shut the door. Barbara begins to *complain* that this could have been avoided and strongly *criticizes* Debbie's careless attitude. Debbie tries to *apologize,* but Barbara *refuses her apology.* Debbie *apologizes* again more emphatically and this time Barbara *accepts the apology* and *requests* that Debbie call the police right away. While waiting for the police, Debbie *expresses regret* that the stereo and television were Barbara's and that nothing of hers was stolen.

The police arrive shortly. The girls *introduce* themselves. The officers *request* that they tell them exactly what happened. The policemen *sympathize* but *caution* the girls that they should take extra precaution in that neighborhood. The girls *promise* that they will from now on. One of the officers *criticizes* the type of lock the girls have and *advises* them to buy a better one. Then the officers say *good-bye.* The girls thank them and *say good-bye.*

The Speeding Ticket

Requesting, commanding, advising, cautioning, promising, apologizing, and sympathizing

Characters: two students
a police officer

Al and Beth are driving to school to take a final exam. Beth *tells* Al to go faster so they won't be late. Al *complains* that it's Beth's fault because she was late getting to his house. Beth *apologizes* and explains that she was trying to review for the exam. Suddenly they hear a siren behind them. Beth *warns* Al to pull over and to be very polite with the police officer. The policeman asks Al why he was in such a hurry. Al *apologizes* and explains that they're late for an exam. The officer *sympathizes* but tells Al to take out his license. Beth *advises* Al to show him the license. Al realizes that he left his wallet at home. He *apologizes* again and explains that he was in a hurry. The officer *cautions* him that driving without a license is illegal. Beth *cautions* him that if they miss the exam she'll never speak to him again. Beth then, very politely, *offers* to drive and shows the officer her license. The officer *agrees* to let them go, just this once, but *cautions* them that if they are ever caught speeding again that they'll go to jail. Al *promises* never to speed again. Al thanks him and wishes him a nice day. Beth moves to the driver's seat. As they slowly drive off to school, Beth *compliments* Al on how polite he was. Al *promises* never to listen to Beth again when she tells him how to drive.